MW01118008

The People's Bible Teachings

CHRISTIAN FREEDOM

Christ Sets Us Free

William E. Fischer

NORTHWESTERN PUBLISHING HOUSE
Milwaukee, Wisconsin

Second printing, 1997

Library of Congress Card 95-71929
Northwestern Publishing House
1250 N. 113th St., Milwaukee, WI 53226-3284
© 1996 by Northwestern Publishing House.
Published 1996
Printed in the United States of America
ISBN 0-8100-0581-6

Table of Contents

Editor's Preface

The People's Bible Teachings is a series of books on all of the main doctrinal teachings of the Bible.

Following the pattern set by The People's Bible series, these books are written especially for laypeople. Theological terms, when used, are explained in everyday language so that people can understand them. The authors show how Christian doctrine is drawn directly from clear passages of Scripture and then how those doctrines apply to people's faith and life. Most importantly, these books show how every teaching of Scripture points to Christ, our only Savior.

The authors of The People's Bible Teachings are parish pastors and professors who have had years of experience teaching the Bible. They are men of scholarship and practical insight.

We take this opportunity to express our gratitude to Professor Leroy Dobberstein of Wisconsin Lutheran Seminary, Mequon, Wisconsin, and Professor Thomas Nass of Martin Luther College, New Ulm, Minnesota, for serving as consultants for this series. Their insights and assistance have been invaluable.

We pray that the Lord will use these volumes to help his people grow in their faith, knowledge, and understanding of his saving teachings, which he has revealed to us in the Bible. To God alone be the glory.

Curtis A. Jahn
Series Editor

Introduction

After I had received the assignment to write a book on Christian freedom, I asked a number of colleagues what they thought of when they heard the expression *Christian freedom*. Invariably they would mention adiaphora, things that God neither commands nor prohibits in the Scriptures. They were right. But there is much more that the Bible teaches about freedom than adiaphora.

Christian freedom refers not only to our sanctification, our life as Christians, but even more importantly, Christian freedom refers, first and foremost, to our justification, the forgiveness of our sins through faith in Christ. A quick glance at the table of contents will indicate to you the biblical truth that our sanctification flows from our justification.

In the Holy Scriptures, God teaches us about Christian freedom for our temporal and eternal good. Such freedom is the prize possession of the Christian and the Christian alone. And I assume that it is yours even before you read this little book. But I pray that by reading it and by meditating on the truths expounded here, you will have a greater appreciation of the God who has created you, his Son who has freed you, and his Spirit who has made Christian freedom your personal possession.

1

Freedom Revealed

Freedom is the watchword of every people, of every age. When we have our freedom, we seem to have everything. Deprived of our freedom, life becomes most difficult.

Words to the song "Born Free," written by Don Black, express it this way:

> Born free, as free as the wind blows,
> as free as the grass grows,
> born free to follow your heart. . . .
>
> Born free, and life is worth living,
> but only worth living
> 'cause you're born free.[1]

Such a philosophy is quite appealing. In the United States, for example, we cherish the freedoms guaranteed us by the Constitution. We are free to choose our leaders and legislators. We are free to protest things that we do not agree with. We are free to live where we want to and to do the kind of work that appeals to us. We are free to worship God according to the dictates of our consciences. Through our government the Lord has given us many freedoms that few nations have enjoyed.

The focus of this book, however, will not be on the temporal freedoms we enjoy but the spiritual freedom we have by God's grace. While we will mention temporal slavery and freedom, on the basis of the Bible we will dwell on the spiritual freedom from slavery that we have through Christ. Such freedom will take center stage in our discussion of Christian freedom.

Created free

Only one person was ever truly born free—Jesus Christ. And the only two other people who ever lived free, if only for a relatively short period of time, were Adam and Eve.

Among all whom God created, our first parents were unique. They were created in the image of God. They had no sin. Their every action was in harmony with God's holy will. Their every word glorified their Creator. Their every thought was pure. They were perfect people created by God to live in his perfect world and take care of it.

God did not have to explain to them the difference between right and wrong. They had God's holy will written in their hearts; his commandments were part of their being. In other words, they knew God and his holy will perfectly.

Having been made in God's image, Adam and Eve were free from sin. Not even the slightest taint of sin could mar their happy life as they enjoyed their God and his creation and each other. They were, therefore, free from all the consequences of sin as we experience them today—sickness and disease and pain and death. They were also free from the power of sin, such as the sins of hatred and lust, which can easily characterize life today.

But they were not only free *from* something; they were also free *for* something. They were free to serve God. Their whole life centered around him. They found joy in obeying every one of his commands. In one way or another, their whole life was a worship of their God. Work was no chore but a joyful service to the Lord. Caring for the Garden of Eden and naming the animals was a tremendous undertaking, but it was done enthusiastically because it was God's will. And when he commanded them not to eat of "the tree of the knowledge of good and evil," God did not impose some burdensome restriction on them; rather, he gave them a special opportunity to demonstrate their love for him in a unique way.

Their only power source for doing good was their Creator. That reflected itself in the life they led. Adam had a perfect, loving relationship with Eve. He treated her with respect and honor, and she lovingly and willingly submitted to his leadership. In time they were to have had a perfect relationship with their children. There would be no need to correct them. These parents would not have spoiled their children. And as the number of people grew, all of them would have lived in perfect harmony. That most certainly was God's intent.

Freedom lost

Since God created people with such freedom in the beginning, why aren't we able to live in that perfect, joyous freedom today? The difference between then and now is the dramatic change that took place when Satan and his cohorts revolted against God in heaven. That revolt happened sometime between the completion of creation and the events that are recorded in Genesis 3. An important part of God's creation was the formation of angels. But some of the "angels . . . did not keep their positions of authority but abandoned their own home [rebelled against God]—these he has kept in darkness, bound with everlasting chains for judgment on the great Day" (Jude 6). Confining the fallen angels does not mean that God stripped them of all their power. For example, Satan was able to take on the form of a serpent, enter the Garden of Eden, and seduce Eve with the words: "Did God really say. . . ?" And the Bible warns us about the "devil's schemes" (Ephesians 6:11); they are intended to lead us into sin and unbelief.

In Adam's wife, Satan found a willing participant. The fruit looked tantalizing, not so much to satisfy an appetite, but as something that would make her be "like God, knowing good and evil" (Genesis 3:5). Later, first Adam and then Eve made alibis. Adam tried to blame Eve for his sin, and Eve tried to blame the serpent (Genesis 3:12,13). But God would not let them shift the blame. He held them fully accountable for what they had done. Our first parents had become thoroughly corrupted by sin. They had lost the holy image of God. They had forfeited their freedom.

A reading of Genesis 3 clearly reveals that they had lost the perfect relationship they had enjoyed with their God. They now feared the God whom they had previously loved with their whole heart. They tried to hide from God when he approached them. So soon they had forgotten that he was all-knowing! They no longer remembered that he was their loving Creator. In other words, they who had been in the image of God now had turned themselves into totally depraved creatures. Or, to put it another way, they who had been perfectly free completely lost their freedom. No longer did they serve God. Now Satan and their sinful nature completely controlled their thoughts and actions.

God made it clear to them that their sin had changed everything. As a consequence of their sin, Adam would have to work by the sweat of his brow to earn a living. And Eve would experience a great deal of pain in what God had intended to be the happiest of occasions—the birth of her children.

As a consequence of their sin, God made certain that they would no longer live in Paradise. He drove them out of the garden and prevented them from eating of the tree of life. Death had now entered the world. All of this was in keeping with God's very words: "You must not eat from the tree of the knowledge of good and evil, for when you eat of it you will surely die" (Genesis 2:17). Their freedom was truly lost.

By this one act of disobedience, our first parents had not only corrupted themselves but the whole human race. Their children were not born in the holy image of God; they were born in the sinful image of their parents. "Adam . . . had a son in his own likeness, in his own image" (Genesis 5:3). This is apparent in the lives of their first two sons, Cain and Abel. Cain gave special evidence of a thoroughly sinful nature. He was jealous of his brother Abel and hated him. And when the opportunity was there, he murdered Abel. Imagine, the first recorded death in the world was fratricide!

Cain and his descendants may have thought they were living free, but they weren't. Rather, they were slaves to their sinful passions and desires. One of them mocked God when he boasted to his wives that he had killed a man. "I have killed a man for wounding me, a young man for injuring me. If Cain is avenged seven times, then Lamech seventy-seven times" (Genesis 4:23,24).

Freedom promised

What a tragic story if it were to have ended with man's fall into sin! Life for every human being would be a hopeless prelude to an eternal judgment. True freedom would be lost forever.

But our gracious God already had a plan to rescue his fallen creatures. He came into the garden that fateful day not merely to confront Adam and Eve personally with their sin, not only to tell them of the dire consequences of their disobedience, but, what is most important, to assure them that he had a plan to rescue them from their tragic dilemma. He would free them from the power of Satan and from the eternal punishment they so justly deserved. He offered a word of hope when he made the promise as he spoke to the serpent: "I will put enmity between you and the woman, and between your offspring and hers; he will crush your head, and you will strike his heel" (Genesis 3:15). With these words God made his first promise of a Savior, a Savior who would come and destroy Satan's power.

God was telling them that they were no longer under the *condemnation* of sin. The Promised One would also free them from sin's *power* so they would no longer be constantly influenced by their sinful nature. The Savior would free them from their sinful passions. Our first parents heard God's promise of a Savior and believed that promise.

But what about the death that God had warned them about if they should disobey him? Didn't they finally die? Most certainly. But the constant fear of death and damnation had been removed. They knew and believed that through their physical death, the Lord would take them into eternal life with unspeakable joys. Once again they knew God as their loving heavenly Father.

Freedom revealed

God's promises of true and eternal spiritual freedom are found in only one place—the Holy Bible. This is not merely another historical document that must be scrutinized for its accuracy. What has been written on the pages of Holy Scripture is truly holy, for God inspired his chosen messengers to record his truth for every generation. "All Scripture is God-breathed" (2 Timothy 3:16). From the first page to the last, the Bible is God's verbally inspired Word. When God tells us in the Bible that we are free, we are free indeed.

This promise and all of those that God makes on the pages of the Bible are there for our learning. The most tragic thing that could happen to any human being would be to deny that God truly loves him, for Jesus promised: "God so loved the world that he gave his one and only Son, that whoever believes in him shall not perish but have eternal life" (John 3:16). In other words, by nature all people have lost their freedom, but now through Christ and his redeeming work, we have been made free.

You may ask: Then how is it that I don't always feel free? The problem is that we have not as yet completely shed the corrupted, sinful nature that enslaved us. It is with us constantly, spoiling our relationship with our God and with one another. Every child of God experiences a daily struggle between his old Adam and his new man. Be glad that is the case, because when we are no longer carrying on this battle, we can be sure that we have lost our true freedom.

Two kinds of freedom

When we search the Scriptures for the word *freedom* or look for events that relate how a person or a nation was freed, we find two kinds of freedom referred to in the Bible: a physical freedom and a spiritual freedom.

Physical freedom is the kind that most people yearn for. The Israelites are a good example of this. At the Lord's direction, a small company of Abraham's descendants went to live in Egypt during a famine, sparing God's chosen people from annihilation. After living 400 years in the land of Goshen, the Israelites had grown into a mighty nation, so great that the pharaoh began to fear these people; so he enslaved them. They had to work under cruel taskmasters; their male children were murdered to weaken them further. Finally, God's people cried out for his mercy. God heard them, and he executed a plan to deliver them. He set his people free from their physical slavery and, under the leadership of Moses, started them on their journey to the Promised Land.

The casual reader of the Bible may imagine that Israel's liberation was the best kind of freedom. In fact, Leon Uris, in his book *Exodus*, states: "Why is this night [the Passover] different from all other nights of the year? This night is different because we celebrate the most important moment in the history of our people. On this night we celebrate their going forth in triumph from slavery into freedom."[2] God mercifully freed Israel from its bondage in Egypt when the Lord killed the firstborn sons of the Egyptians and passed over the blood-stained doorframes of the Israelites. But for the true Israelites, the celebration of the Passover would mean much more. God gave them this meal to remind them of the Lamb who would free them from spiritual and eternal slavery.

The Bible contains other references to physical freedom. In one of God's laws given to Israel, God commands: "If a fellow Hebrew, a man or a woman, sells himself to you and serves you six years, in the seventh year you must let him go free" (Deuteronomy 15:12). The Lord instructed King Zedekiah through the prophet Jeremiah that "everyone was to free his Hebrew slaves, both male and female; no one was to hold a fellow Jew in bondage" (Jeremiah 34:9).

It is usually easy to determine whether the word *freedom* is used in the physical or the spiritual sense in the Bible. The context will make it clear.

Secular history often relates events of slavery and freedom. The bloodiest war in the history of our country was fought over the issue of slavery and freedom. The first amendment of our Constitution speaks of the freedoms that are guaranteed to every citizen of the United States: freedom of speech, freedom of religion, freedom of the press. As much as we as Christians may cherish these freedoms and regard them as gifts from God, they are as nothing when they are compared to the freedom we have in Christ. The one is physical; the other is spiritual. The one is temporal; the other is eternal.

Yes, the Bible alone reveals the only kind of freedom that really matters. Only in the Bible are we able to learn how our sins are forgiven and why God has accepted us as his children. Only the Bible unfolds God's gracious plan of salvation from promise to fulfillment. The wisest men in the world could use their collective wisdom and still not answer the question correctly: How can I be truly free? For "It is written: 'No eye has seen, no ear has heard, no mind has conceived what God has prepared for those who love him'—but God has revealed it to us by his Spirit" (1 Corinthians 2:9,10). And it was the Holy Spirit who inspired men to write the books of the Bible. "The holy Scriptures . . . are able to make you wise for salvation through faith in Christ Jesus. All Scripture is God-breathed and is useful for teaching, rebuking, correcting and training in right-eousness" (2 Timothy 3:15,16). The Scriptures are useful for teaching what true freedom is all about.

Free will

The Bible also has something to say about that which is no longer free—man's will.

God had created our first parents with a free will in all matters of life. Their free will was in perfect harmony with the will of their Creator. They had the choice between obeying God and breaking his commandments. But that changed after the fall. No longer could they choose to believe in God and follow his commands in a way that was pleasing to him. They were spiritually dead. No longer could they, by their own will, make choices that pleased God. What was true of Adam and Eve after they sinned is true of everyone today before his or her conversion (see Ephesians 2:1).

Many claim that all people have by nature at least a spark of spiritual life in them. They imagine that they can consciously will themselves to be a Christian or at least contribute something to their conversion. For those who believe that they have made a decision for Christ of their own free will, Jesus reminds them: "No one can come to me unless the Father who sent me draws him" (John 6:44).

It is true that in earthly matters people do have free will to a certain extent: what to eat and wear, where to live, what kind of work to do. But because of the sinful nature, no one has the free will to believe in Christ. In spiritual matters, God does the choosing and calling. That is why we confess in Luther's explanation to the Third Article: "I believe that I cannot by my own thinking or choosing believe in Jesus Christ, my Lord, or come to him. But the Holy Spirit has called me by the gospel."

Once conversion has occurred, God gives the Christian the will or desire to obey the commands he has revealed in the Bible. The Scriptures state: "It is God who works in you to will and to act according to his good purpose" (Philippians 2:13).

If anyone imagines that he has spiritual freedom and does not believe God's Word, he is only deceiving himself. If anyone is searching for a freedom that really frees, he will find it on the pages of Holy Scripture. There alone true freedom has been revealed.

2

Freedom Declared

On January 1, 1863, President Abraham Lincoln declared free all slaves residing in the territory in rebellion against the federal government of the United States. This Emancipation Proclamation actually freed few people. It did not apply to slaves in border states fighting on the Union side, nor did it affect slaves in southern areas already under Union control. That proclamation did not free many slaves. But there was one declaration that did.

Many years before the United States was founded, the almighty God declared all people free from the guilt of their sins. The Bible calls his declaration "justification." "[Christ] was raised to life for our justification" (Romans 4:25).

The meaning of justification

The word *justify* is found throughout the Scriptures. In the Old Testament the prophet Isaiah wrote: "He who vindicates [justifies] me is near. Who then will bring charges against me? Let us face each other! Who is my accuser? Let him confront me!" (50:8).

In the New Testament the apostle Paul wrote to the Romans: "[All] are justified freely by his grace through the redemption that came by Christ Jesus" (3:24).

But what does it mean that God justifies? The word *justify* is a judicial term. It means to declare righteous. Since it is used as a legal term in the Bible, it can best be described by a court scene. The accused is brought before the judge; the evidence is presented; the verdict is rendered.

In a human court the verdict is based on the best evidence available. If a person has committed a crime and if the prosecutor has presented irrefutable evidence, the individual is declared guilty either by a jury or a judge. Then a sentence is given, based on the severity of the crime. If there is insufficient evidence or if the accused is able to demonstrate that he did not commit the crime, he is freed from the accusation that was brought against him. This is justice as we commonly understand it.

The Bible describes God as the judge of heaven and earth. "Will not the Judge of all the earth do right?" (Genesis 18:25). But what kind of judgment does he pronounce on the world? On the sixth day, when he surveyed all that he had created, "God saw all that he had made, and it was very good" (Genesis 1:31). And that judgment included our first parents. But their one sin changed all of that. When they ate of the forbidden fruit, they not only corrupted themselves but the whole human race. "The result of one trespass was condemnation for all men" (Romans 5:18). What a horrible fate awaited us all, until a just but gracious God intervened! "So also the result of one act of righteousness was justification that brings life for all men" (Romans 5:18).

That "one act of righteousness" was carried out at the Father's direction and by his only-begotten Son. According to God's eternal plan and because of all that Christ did, the just God was able to make a declaration of freedom and forgiveness to a sin-cursed and hell-bound world of humanity. And that proclamation by the holy judge was simply: You are innocent; you are freed from the condemnation of your sins. In the biblical sense, then, justification is God declaring the sinner forgiven. It is the judge's verdict of acquittal.

Persons justified

And for whom was God's gracious proclamation intended? Was it for those who seemed to lead a respectable life? Was it only for those who believed and worshiped the true and living God? Paul gives us a clear answer when he writes: "God was reconciling *the world* to himself in Christ, not counting men's sins against them" (2 Corinthians 5:19).

Does the word *world* as Paul uses it in this Bible passage mean *everyone*? What about Cain or Judas or their present-day counterparts? What about those who blaspheme God with their words and actions their entire lives? Has God justified them? They most certainly are included in the world of mankind that has been declared justified by God. When Jesus told Nicodemus, "God so loved the world," he did not put any restrictions on the number and the kinds of people in the world who are loved by God.

Once when Jesus was visiting his hometown of Naza-reth, he attended the service at the local synagogue on the Sabbath day. When he was invited to read the Scripture lesson for the day and to say a few words, he read what Isa-iah had said about him over 700 years before. "The Spirit of the Lord is on me, because he has anointed me to preach good news to the poor. He has sent me to proclaim freedom for the prisoners" (Luke 4:18). In other words, his heavenly Father had called him into his special ministry "to proclaim freedom for the prisoners."

Some may wonder when and how Jesus ever freed pris-oners. When we read the history of the early church, we learn that many people were put into prison because they were followers of Christ. Even John the Baptist, Christ's forerunner, ended up in prison and was executed. But he died a free man in the spiritual sense of the word. For Jesus declares freedom to those who are prisoners of sin and Satan.

Although Jesus had not as yet suffered, died, and arisen when he declared freedom to spiritual prisoners, he could make a proclamation of freedom as if his redeeming work had already been accomplished. The "prisoners" are all those under the servitude of sin, and that describes all peo-ple by nature. The good news is that God has forgiven all people all of their transgressions because of who Jesus is— God and man—and because of what Jesus did: he lived a perfect life and finally died the death of the damned.

God's act of reconciling the world to himself was com-pletely one-sided. He did not wait for mankind to "prove" itself, because he knew that was impossible. Sin had com-pletely estranged the whole human race from God.

As a gracious God he did not put any conditions on his justification of an alienated world. He did not say, "If you live up to my commands, then I will justify you." He did not even say, "I will forgive you *if* you believe in me." His universal justification stands, whether people believe it or not.

Some would have us believe that God justifies only those who believe in him. But that would rob us of God's grace and the blessed truth of our—and, yes, everyone's— justification. Such a teaching would begin to cast doubt on whether or not we are worthy enough to be included in God's declaration of love and freedom and forgiveness. It would exclude some people from the "world" that Jesus had referred to in John 3:16.

Justification was not an arbitrary pronouncement of for- giveness by God. He did not close his eyes to all the sin that has filled the world since the Fall and will continue to be committed until the end of time. God did not coun- sel with himself: "I could never send anyone to hell." That would contradict his threat: "Whoever does not believe will be condemned" (Mark 16:16). He is a just God, and his justice had to be satisfied completely. He knew that none of us could ever stand righteous in his sight on our own. He knew there was only one verdict he could render and be a righteous judge: Guilty.

But he had a plan, a plan that would satisfy his just demands and also demonstrate his love for fallen man- kind. From eternity, divine counsel decreed that the sec- ond person in the Trinity would become man and do what all the other human beings could not do for themselves: live a life in perfect harmony with God's holy will and die as an atoning sacrifice for sin. Only then could all sinners be redeemed. That is why Christ took our place under the law, obeyed it perfectly, and became sin for us. And that is why the righteous judge declares all people righteous.

What a great comfort this blessed truth is! We have moments of doubt, times when we wonder if God really loves us. We might even ask ourselves: Is God punishing me for some sin? Am I being good enough? Is my faith in him strong enough? But these are questions that we need not be asking ourselves. For our loving God has *already* declared us forgiven for the sake of his Son and his redemption. What good news for troubled hearts!

This is the saving message that God wants all to hear. Those whom the Spirit has called to faith have also been called to be Christ's witnesses. We want to always keep in mind the blessed truth that all those with whom we have any contact have already been redeemed by Christ and been declared forgiven. That truth is a tremendous motivation for doing mission work. No matter to whom our missionaries talk, no matter what that person's past has been, no matter how hopeless he or she may seem to be, the missionary proclaims the gospel to that person, telling the sinner that though his or her sins are as scarlet, through Christ they are as white as snow (Isaiah 1:18). In your witness be assured that God wants all people in your world to hear that Christ loves them and has freely and fully forgiven them their sins.

By faith alone

But does this mean that all people are right with God, have received his gracious forgiveness, and will go to heaven? Not at all. How, then, are we personally justified? How does God's gracious pardon and acquittal become our very own?

Many people imagine that if they are going to "get right" with God, they are going to have to do it on their own. This has been true from the earliest times. Paul described the unbelieving Israelites in this way: "Since they did not know the righteousness that comes from God and sought to establish their own, they did not submit to God's righteousness" (Romans 10:3).

Israel was God's chosen people, selected by him to be the bearer of his promises, which included the promise of a Savior. God established his law among them. A primary function of his law was to remind them of their sinful depravity, which would make them long for his mercy. But they imagined that their outward "obedience" made them righteous; they tried to establish their own righteousness before God and thereby rejected the righteousness that God graciously offered them through the promised Messiah. In other words, they, like so many people, tried to save themselves. As a result, they were not personally justified.

The Pharisees of Jesus' day were good examples of self-righteous people. They were not satisfied with "obeying" God's Old Testament ordinances, but they prided themselves in keeping the many traditions that they had developed over the years. They did not feel, therefore, that they needed a Savior from sin, and they became some of the most bitter opponents of Christ.

There is no greater temptation for those who profess to be Christians than self-righteousness. We can so easily deceive ourselves into thinking how good we are when we compare ourselves with others in this ungodly world. We can so easily confess our faith in Christ while, at the same time, clinging to the notion that who we are and what we are doing, in part at least, are making us right with God. But the Bible speaks of "the blessedness of the man to whom God credits righteousness apart from works" (Romans 4:6).

Some people will always twist the Scriptures in order to harmonize them with their own personal beliefs, in order to justify themselves and their sinful actions. For example, when Greg Louganis publicly acknowledged that he had AIDS, he claimed that he felt as if a great burden had been lifted from his soul. Louganis was an Olympic champion, one of the best divers ever to step on a springboard. For years after he was diagnosed with the illness, he told very few that he was HIV-positive. He even contemplated suicide. And then he went public, revealing that he was a homosexual and that he had the dreaded disease. Reports said he often quoted the biblical phrase "The truth will set you free."[3] Yes, he imagined that he was set free from guilt and shame by simply telling the people the truth about himself. Oh that he would learn, before it is too late, that God has declared him forgiven and that faith in Christ alone will set him free!

Before his Damascus encounter with Christ, Saul, who became the apostle Paul, was convinced that he was "free," that he was right with God. He was a Pharisee of the first order. He was convinced that he was working himself into heaven and was doing a special service for God by persecuting the Christians. He thought that if anyone could be saved by obeying God's law, he could. But the moment he came to faith in Christ, he knew that he was chosen to be saved only by God's grace. That is why he could confess, "By the grace of God I am what I am" (1 Corinthians 15:10). And that is why he wrote: "Not having a righteousness of my own that comes from the law, but that which is through faith in Christ—the righteousness that comes from God and is by faith" (Philippians 3:9).

Our righteousness truly does come from God. He gave up that which was closest to his heart for our salvation—

his beloved Son. He sent him into the world; he put him under the law; he sent him to the cross. And when he raised him from the dead, he declared all sinners righteous.

Faith alone justifies

But God's grace was not finished; he left nothing to chance. He knew that this marvelous gift would come only to those who believed in Christ, and he knew that none of us had the power to work faith in our own hearts. So he sent us his Holy Spirit to convert us through the gospel. And through that faith we are justified; we have been truly freed from sin and its curse, from death and its fear, from Satan and his power. We have been made right with God.

Some have struggled with the doctrine that we are saved through faith alone, without the works of the law. Some have even claimed that faith is something that we must work in our own hearts. Don't we have to choose Christ by asking him to come into our hearts as many TV evangelists invite their hearers to do? Jesus, however, reminded his disciples, "You did not choose me, but I chose you" (John 15:16). And the Bible also says, "No one can say, 'Jesus is Lord,' except by the Holy Spirit" (1 Corinthians 12:3).

After his conversion Luther held fast to the biblical truth that we are saved by God's grace alone, through faith alone. And he emphasized the *alone* to refute those who tried to add works to faith and salvation. Speaking of how faith alone saves a person, Luther stated: "See to it that you do not add any comment to these words and that you do not try to make them better than Christ has made them. They have said that one must understand them like this: 'He that believeth (understand: "and does good works") shall be saved.' Who has commanded them to make this addition? Do you suppose the Holy Spirit is so stupid that He could not have added these words? So they have completely obscured, nay, they have perverted, this noble passage with this addition. See to it, therefore, that you allow no one to make an addition for you, but that you stay with the words just as they read and that you understand them in this way: 'He that believeth shall be saved' without his merit or any work."[4]

Faith has been aptly described as the hand that receives God's gift of salvation. A beggar who holds out his hand and receives a gift would not brag that it was his beautiful hand that motivated the giver. The giver's compassion would have been the only reason he wanted to help out that poor person.

Another illustration may help us understand what faith is and its place in our salvation. If a friend of yours suddenly gave you a check for a million dollars, you would probably reason that he is playing some joke on you. Since you were not aware of the fact that he had suddenly been the beneficiary of a large inheritance, you would promptly rip up the check. Your lack of trust would rob you of becoming a millionaire. On the other hand, if you had complete confidence in the integrity of this faithful friend and deposited the check, your trust would have been rewarded. Yes, God "rewards" us for the faith he has given us, by granting us an eternal peace and joy. And his reward is a reward of grace.

By grace alone

To faith alone the Scriptures add *by grace alone*. "It is by grace you have been saved, through faith—and this not from yourselves, it is the gift of God" (Ephesians 2:8).

Grace is another word for love. But when it is used in the Bible, it refers to love that is totally undeserved. When we confess that we are saved by grace alone, we are saying that there is nothing in our being or our character or our doing that has prompted God to love us and declare us to be his very own. Grace means that God has a pure and unconditional love for us.

The doctrine of justification is the rock foundation of our Christian faith. It gives true meaning to the word *grace*. And justification underscores the truth, "Where sin increased, grace increased all the more" (Romans 5:20). And all those who are convinced that they have been justified through faith by God's grace alone have experienced true Christian freedom.

3

Freedom from the Law

John's case history was discussed in a Bible class. He had grown up in a devout Roman Catholic family. He had diligently practiced the rites of the Roman Catholic Church that he believed would bring him salvation. But he was greatly troubled in his conscience, even though he led a respectable life. He knew in his heart that he had violated God's law many times.

In his search for peace, John came into contact with Mormon people. They were kind and friendly and seemed to be at peace with themselves because of their religion. He thought that the Mormon religion had the answers he was looking for, and he became a Mormon.

A few months later he went to Las Vegas on his first Mormon mission. He had been taught that this was one of the steps to godhood. He went on a second mission, and later he was married in the Mormon temple.

John became involved in some of the highest rituals in the Salt Lake City temple. He was baptized many times for those already dead, believing that he was helping them up the ladder toward godhood.

Still, John had a troubled conscience. He had a gnawing feeling that he was not earning God's favor; he just was not doing enough. He studied Mormon doctrine more diligently, but still found no peace. Why not?

Enslaved by the law

Without realizing it, he was enslaved by the law, both God's and man's. He endured what had happened to Dr. Martin Luther 500 years before. Luther had spent the first 30 years of his life enslaved by the law. He had been taught to obey the law of God and the laws of the Roman Catholic Church in order to get right with God. When he was in a monastery, he did everything that was demanded of him and more. Later he became a priest and a professor at the University at Wittenberg. Even though he led an exemplary life, his sins still bothered him.

Both John (the Mormon) and Luther had experienced what Saint Paul describes in Romans, "Don't you know that when you offer yourselves to someone to obey him as slaves, you are slaves to the one whom you obey?" (6:16). If someone is trying to find peace with God by obeying the law, he thereby becomes a slave of the law.

Paul knew what it meant to be a slave of the law. He had been schooled in Old Testament Law and Jewish traditions by some of the finest teachers. He acknowledged, "According to the strictest sect of our religion, I [Paul] lived as a Pharisee" (Acts 26:5). He was convinced that by his daily duties and acts of obedience, he was earning God's favor and securing his place in heaven. He was a slave to the law.

And, with but few exceptions, so were all of the Jews during New Testament times. Jesus' most bitter opponents were the Jews in general and the Pharisees in particular. "To the Jews who had believed him, Jesus said, 'If you hold to my teaching, you are really my disciples. Then you will know the truth, and the truth will set you free.' They answered him, 'We are Abraham's descendants and have never been slaves of anyone. How can you say that we shall be set free?'" (John 8:31-33). The Jews imagined that they were free, both politically and spiritually.

Often those who are slaves to the law don't even realize they are in bondage. They imagine they can justify themselves. However, the Bible says, "Now we know that whatever the law says, it says to those who are under the law, so that every mouth may be silenced and the whole world held accountable to God" (Romans 3:19). Since everyone is under the law, everyone is silenced by the law. No one can say even one word in his defense, claiming that he has kept God's law.

Cursed by the law

The tragedy is that those who have been enslaved by the law, who imagine they are right with God because of who they are and what they are doing, are silenced when they have to give account to the holy God. The law has not only enslaved them, but before God they stand condemned, for "all who rely on observing the law are under a curse, for it is written: 'Cursed is everyone who does not continue to do everything written in the Book of the Law'" (Galatians 3:10).

This curse of God places us all in the same predicament, for none of us can claim perfect obedience to God's law. The day hardly begins, and we have a sinful thought, speak a careless word, and violate God's holy will. We daily confess with the apostle Paul, "I know that nothing good lives in me, that is, in my sinful nature. For I have the desire to do what is good, but I cannot carry it out. For what I do is not the good I want to do; no, the evil I do not want to do—this I keep on doing" (Romans 7:18,19). Paul is speaking as a Christian who realizes that he has a sinful flesh. That same kind of sinful flesh also clings to us. And we cannot comfort ourselves by imagining that the sins we commit are in some way balanced by the good that we do. God's justice is not satisfied that way.

God's plan for our freedom

How, then, can we or anyone escape from the slavery and condemnation of the law? Only by looking to our gracious God and learning what he has planned for us, yes, for all mankind. It didn't take God long to let our first parents know what the consequences of their sin would mean for them and their children. They had no sooner made excuses for their sin than the Lord promised that one would come and redeem them, and he kept repeating and enhancing this promise throughout the Old Testament times through his prophets. They proclaimed God's promises for thousands of years. "But when the time had fully come, God sent his Son, born of a woman, born under law, to redeem those under law, that we might receive the full rights of sons" (Galatians 4:4,5).

What does it mean that Jesus was born under the law? It means that the Father placed his Son under the law, imposed it upon him, and expected him to keep it perfect-ly when he sent Jesus into the world.

Jesus had always been the Son of God. When he was conceived by the Holy Spirit in the womb of the virgin Mary and was born, Jesus became man in every sense of the word except that he was born without sin. And when the Father sent his Son into the world, he put him under the law. God, in effect, said to his Son: "Every law I have given to my people, I am also giving you to obey. I want you to do something that they have not done—keep the law perfectly. And I want you to keep my commandments for every sinner." When Mary gave birth to Jesus, he was "born under law." That means that Jesus was obliged to keep every command God gave to his people.

From early on Jesus lived in conformity to God's will, a will he had imposed upon his people Israel. As an infant, Jesus was presented to the Lord and was circumcised according to the law. In his youth he honored his legal father and mother according to the Fourth Command-ment; he gladly heard and learned God's Word, according to the Third Commandment. As an adult, he relieved the suffering of many people and took care of their bodily needs, in keeping with the Fifth Commandment. And on two occasions, when he was baptized and when he was transfigured, his Father clearly stated: "This is my Son, whom I love; with him I am well pleased" (Matthew 3:17; 17:5). His Father was pleased because his Son did what we haven't done—he kept God's commandments perfectly—no careless word, no evil thought, no sinful act.

Freedom secured

Why did Christ lead a perfect life and die an innocent death? He did it to redeem those who are under the law but have repeatedly broken it. To redeem means to buy back, to free from. Today we use the word *ransom* to describe the demands of terrorists who hold a person hostage. Without Christ, the sinner is held hostage to God's law and to all of its demands. For the Israelites, that included every ordinance that God had given his people. God condemned people for even the slightest infraction of his rules; he cursed them. "For it is written: 'Cursed is everyone who does not continue to do everything written in the Book of the Law'" (Galatians 3:10).

Christ, therefore, came into the world to free sinners from the demands of the law and its curse. Some experienced such freedom during Jesus' ministry. The Pharisee Nicodemus came to Jesus because he knew that there was something special about this teacher, and he wanted to find out what it was. From Jesus' own lips he heard how the curse and slavery of the law were removed: "God so loved the world that he gave his one and only Son" (John 3:16). Later Nicodemus boldly professed his freedom when he assisted in the burial of Jesus.

Freedom challenged

The apostle Paul's special calling from God was to proclaim the good news primarily to Gentiles. On his first missionary journey he traveled to Galatia, preaching the gospel of Jesus Christ, and many were converted.

But the messenger of light was followed by men of darkness. They came to those congregations that Paul had founded and belittled Paul and his ministry. They posed as followers of Christ, but they had a different message. They said: "Yes, you must believe in Christ. But that does not mean that you need not keep the Old Testament ordinances that God gave to his people. If you really want to

be Christians, you should be circumcised and should perform all of the ceremonies God gave to the Jews."

These false prophets were leading the Galatians back to
the slavery of the law and its curse. For they, like Catholi-
cism after them, taught that faith *plus works* will get you
into heaven.

When Paul heard the errors the Galatians were being
taught, the doctrine that would rob them of their Christian freedom, he wrote them a letter. He reminded them,
"All who rely on observing the law are under a curse"
(Galatians 3:10) and "you who are trying to be justified by
law have been alienated from Christ" (Galatians 5:4).
Again and again he assured them that sinners are saved by
God's grace alone through faith in Christ. Only through
him were they free children of God.

The Galatians had been infected with a very enticing
error. We, too, can succumb to such a damning teaching.
How easily we confess that we are Christians. How nicely
we can make all the right confessions. But at the same
time, our sinful flesh and Satan try to lead us astray by
telling us to trust in ourselves rather than in him alone
who has redeemed us. Christ alone, by his perfect life and
his innocent death, has freed us from the curse and condemnation of the law.

A sinner freed

Remember John, the former Catholic and Mormon, the
man who could not find real peace with God no matter
how hard he tried? This is the rest of his story.

He and his family moved to Denver, where a caring
Christian introduced John to his Lutheran pastor. A good
relationship developed between the pastor and this young
family. They frequently attended the Lutheran church ser-

vices, and the pastor had private Bible study in the couple's home. They heard the good news that they were saved by God's grace alone without any merit on their part. They learned about all that God promised and all that Christ did. Through the Word of God, the Holy Spirit touched their hearts. They found their peace with God. For the first time, their consciences were free.

John could not keep this good news to himself. He became an active evangelist for the congregation in the community, and he took a special interest in Mormons, in those who were enslaved by the law.

Luther's slavery to the law ended during one of his Bible studies. He struggled with the expression "righteousness of God" in the first chapter of Romans. In those words he could only see God as a righteous judge, showing his wrath and punishing sin, until one day Luther read and meditated on the words, "The righteous will live *by faith*" (Romans 1:17). Later, in describing his conversion, he stated, "This passage of Paul appeared to me as the gate to Paradise." For the first time in his life, he was freed from the law and a troubled conscience, knowing that through faith in Christ alone the sinner becomes righteous.

Freedom easily abused

Some have claimed that teaching salvation by grace alone through faith will encourage the hearers to disregard God's law and live in sin. Won't they be tempted to have a complete disregard for the Ten Commandments when they learn that they are freed from the law?

This contention is hardly anything new. In fact, Paul addressed that false notion in his letter to the Romans. "The law was added so that the trespass might increase.

But where sin increased, grace increased all the more, so that, just as sin reigned in death, so also grace might reign through righteousness to bring eternal life through Jesus Christ our Lord. What shall we say, then? Shall we go on sinning so that grace may increase? By no means! We died to sin; how can we live in it any longer?" (Romans 5:20–6:2).

As was mentioned above, the law was first written in men's hearts, but because of a perverse human nature, God's immutable will was no longer clearly known. That is why God wrote the Ten Commandments on two tables of stone for Moses to give to his people. God wanted all to have a clear understanding of what his holy will is.

But how does the giving of the law cause sin to increase? The law more clearly reveals to sinful mankind how they are violating God's commands. The better we know God's will for our lives, the more conscious we are of our sins. How comforting to know that "where sin increased, grace increased all the more."

But again, would not those who hear of God's grace assume that, being free from the demands of the law for their salvation, they could live freely without any restraints of the law, disregarding even what God had originally written in their hearts? Wouldn't they believe that they were free to live as they pleased? Some might even go so far as to think that by their sinning they are giving God an even greater opportunity to show the sinner his love. Paul answered emphatically, "By no means! We died to sin [when we came to faith in Christ]; how can we live in it any longer?"

However, the notion that the Christian may now completely ignore God's law still spooks around in the church that clearly proclaims Christ's gracious redeeming work.

For example, there was a young boy in a confirmation class who had lived in one foster home after another because he was most difficult to handle. A middle-aged couple had taken him into their home because they wanted to serve Christ in some special way. They joined a congregation that had a Lutheran elementary school because they wanted to give him a Christian education. The boy was instructed along with the other seventh and eighth graders.

One day his foster parents corrected the boy for some offense, and he defended himself by saying, "That's all right. The pastor said that Jesus was punished for all my sins." The parents mentioned the incident to the pastor, and he promised to speak to him. He pointed out to the boy that what he had confessed was true about Jesus. Jesus had taken away the guilt of all his sins. But he also reminded him of what he had also learned from the Bible. It was summed up in Luther's explanation to the Second Article of the Apostles' Creed. "He [Christ] has redeemed me . . . that I should be his own, and live under him in his kingdom, and serve him in everlasting righteousness, innocence, and blessedness." This living under Christ begins the moment someone trusts in him as Savior; this serving him begins now, not only sometime in the future.

Later, the boy's foster parents reported that he came home with a different attitude. Apparently he knew that the freedom he had through Christ was not an excuse for continuing to live in sin. Such is the power of the Word of truth that frees us from the law and for service.

We also may be tempted, as some are, to use our freedom from the law as a cover-up for wickedness. For example, some have claimed that since abortion is a sin, they have the right to employ any kind of civil disobedience to protest the killing of unborn babies. But in obeying God's law we are not forced to break the laws of the land, for God has clearly told us in the Scriptures that we are to obey those whom he has chosen to rule over us. The only exception to this rule is when someone in authority commands us to do something that God clearly forbids. In such a case our only response can be, "We must obey God rather than men!" (Acts 5:29).

God truly wants us to enjoy the freedom that we have found in Christ. He wants us to exercise it to the fullest. "Live as free men," the apostle Peter encourages us. But he also warns, "Do not use your freedom as a cover-up for evil; live as servants of God" (1 Peter 2:16). In the same vein, the apostle Paul writes: "You, my brothers, were called to be free. But do not use your freedom to indulge the sinful nature; rather, serve one another in love" (Galatians 5:13).

Two Christians in the early church tried to play the cover-up game. God had not told his New Testament believers how much they should give to the church. However, the members of that early congregation in Jerusalem were so filled with faith and love that they shared with each other everything they had. Ananias and his wife Sapphira claimed they were giving their all when they brought a generous gift to the apostles. Actually, they were using their freedom of Christian stewardship to cover up the fact that they were holding back a portion of their money. God exposed their lying and hypocrisy and killed them on the spot (Acts 5).

Rest for our souls

While Jesus himself warned, "Be afraid of the One who can destroy both soul and body in hell" (Matthew 10:28), he knew that such fear of God would never draw sinners closer to him. That is why he offered this gracious invitation, "Come to me, all you who are weary and burdened, and I will give you rest. Take my yoke upon you and learn from me, for I am gentle and humble in heart, and you will find rest for your souls. For my yoke is easy and my burden is light" (Matthew 11:28-30).

The burden that Jesus was speaking about was the law that God had given to Moses and the Israelites. It became such a heavy load for the Jews to bear because they were being taught, and they believed, that only by obeying the law could they be right with God. But now Jesus wanted them to come to him, for he had removed that burden from them. He was keeping the law in their stead, and his obedience would eventually take him to the cross. Thereby he offered them true rest for their souls.

We have peace and rest for our souls because we believe that Jesus is not just another lawgiver, but he is our law-fulfiller. Now only through him do we find our way to our loving heavenly Father; only through him have we received complete pardon for all of our transgressions; and only through him is our eternal home secured. And he assures us that his yoke is easy and his burden is light.

Yes, through Christ we see God's law in a different light. As children of God we enjoy doing his will. Now we will be able to say with Paul, "In my inner being I delight in God's law" (Romans 7:22).

Such is the experience of those who have been freed from the law. The law of God is no longer a burden, for those who live in daily repentance of their sins with a firm trust in Jesus Christ as their Savior find their joy in life doing his bidding. His law has become for them a lamp lighting the path they walk in this life.

All this is ours because Christ has freed his people from the law.

4

Freedom from Sin

"Sold."

The auctioneer was brisk and businesslike, and the word he spoke so matter-of-factly carried clearly across the crowd gathered before the steps of old Wetherburn's Tavern. The place—Williamsburg, Virginia. The year—1994. It was a reenactment of the selling of slaves that had occurred in colonial Williamsburg. Its protesters called it dehumanizing; its defenders claimed they were putting a face on history, so that people could see and hear and feel what had gone on in the past.

The Bible records incidents when believers possessed slaves. As children of God, however, they did not treat their servants harshly but in accord with the general principle: Love your neighbor as yourself. The apostle Paul

47

converted to Christianity a runaway slave by the name of Onesimus, and then he urged him to return to his master, who was also a Christian. In his letter to Philemon, Paul lovingly appealed that the slave be treated as a fellow believer, for they all knew that there was a much worse slavery from which they had been freed—the slavery of sin. Yes, Onesimus, the slave, was freed when he heard and believed the gospel of Jesus Christ. He was freed from sin, Satan, and death.

Different words for sin

What does it mean to be freed from sin? Before we can answer that question, we must have a clear understanding of what sin is.

We are living at a time when there is no longer a clear distinction between right and wrong. As a result, many are living in sin while at the same time they imagine that they are free to live their lives as they see fit. In the Bible, God does not mince any words. He plainly tells us what he wants people to do and what he forbids. And he uses different words in the Scriptures to describe disobedience against him.

The word *sin* itself very often means to miss the mark. We may aim in the right direction of God's will, but we will never hit the bull's eye. No matter how hard we try, we always miss the mark. In fact, we miss the target altogether with our sin.

The word *transgression* is also used to describe our disobedience to God. In describing the suffering of the promised Savior, the prophet wrote, "He was pierced for our transgressions" (Isaiah 53:5). *Transgression* means crossing the forbidden line. Because of our sinful nature, we are always crossing the line at which God has posted the sign: KEEP OUT.

Another synonym for sin is *iniquity*. "He was crushed for our iniquities" (Isaiah 53:5) is one way of explaining what Christ has done for us. The word *iniquity* means failing to measure up perfectly. We are only deceiving ourselves when we compare who we are and what we are doing to what others are doing, for we will always select someone who does not measure up as we like to think we do. But the comparison that God wants us to make is not with other sinful, human beings but with him. He is holy, and we are not. Thus, a true evaluation of our person causes us to come to the conclusion that we haven't measured up and we never will because our life is filled with iniquity.

Origin of sin

And where does our sin come from? Did it come from outside influences as we were growing up? Certainly enough of those exist today. Even the finest Christian homes have been exposed to every kind of ungodliness through TV. While sin is easily multiplied in so many ways, these evil influences are not the origin of our personal sin.

Rather, sin has been in the fabric of our very being from the moment we were conceived. When we see newborn babies, they seem so innocent that we can easily reason that they haven't lived long enough to sin. We might also conclude that at the beginning of our lifetime we also enjoyed such innocence. But our reason and even our eyes easily deceive us in spiritual matters. That is why God was pleased to reveal to us not only how the world began but also how sin came to infect the whole human race.

God gave our first parents a perfect life and a beautiful home in which to live. When God created them, he wrote his law into their hearts so that they had perfect knowledge of his will, and, in addition, he gave them a special command that would enable them to demonstrate their love for him. He forbade them to eat of the "tree of the knowledge of good and evil," but they disobeyed him and immediately corrupted their whole being with sin. Breaking one of his commandments means violating all of them.

That first sin not only thoroughly corrupted Adam and Eve, but it was also the origin of all sinning in the world. "Just as sin entered the world through one man, and death through sin, and in this way death came to all men, because all sinned" (Romans 5:12). David knew the source of his sin. "Surely I was sinful at birth, sinful from the time my mother conceived me" (Psalms 51:5). He had inherited his sinful nature from his parents. And so have we, for "flesh gives birth to flesh" (John 3:6). Since we are sinful flesh, we are passing our sin down to the next generation.

Consequences of sin

Let us not imagine that our sins, as insignificant as they might seem to us, don't matter much. God had told Adam that if he would eat of the forbidden fruit, he would die. He did die, and we will also die unless judgment day comes first. Death is the consequence of sin.

Sin brought with it God's condemnation. Sin makes God angry, so angry that he has reserved a place called hell for those who are disobedient. In other words, God threatens sinners with eternal damnation, and untold millions will hear Christ say on the Last Day, "Depart from me, you who are cursed, into the eternal fire prepared for the devil and his angels" (Matthew 25:41). Yes, we too deserve to hear these words from the lips of our Savior, for sin has brought God's curse on us all.

Slavery of sin

To heighten his warning against sin, Jesus taught that sin has a slavish hold on people. "I tell you the truth, everyone who sins is a slave to sin" (John 8:34). What does Jesus mean? Is he saying that *we* are slaves to sin? We are if we are living apart from God, if we have rejected Jesus as our Savior. Jesus was speaking to those and about those who did not believe in him. He told them: You imagine that you are free. You are proud to be a descendant of Abraham. You think your natural birth and your good works have made you right with God. But they haven't. In reality, you are slaves to sin.

That is mighty strong language. It is hardly the way to win friends and influence people. But Jesus was not running in a popularity contest. He had come to seek and to save that which was lost. He came to call sinners to repentance. And until sinners see their lost condition, they will never know Jesus as their Savior.

The apostle Paul uses the expression "slaves to sin" (Romans 6:6) in describing how all people are by nature. Both Jesus and the apostle are using the word *slave* to describe someone who has no power of his own. He is completely under the control of someone else; he has to do that person's bidding constantly. That aptly describes the power sin has over the individual, and the Scriptures offer some classic examples of sin-slavery.

Cain is the first person who demonstrated that sin had complete control of him. He was jealous of his brother Abel and hated him. In spite of God's warning, he lured Abel into a situation so that he could kill him. After he murdered Abel, he felt sorry for himself but not for his sin. The Bible says, "Cain went out from the LORD's presence" (Genesis 4:16). That is another way of saying that he remained an unbeliever, a slave of sin.

David is a good example of how a believer's sinful passions can get the best of him. First he saw Bathsheba; then he seduced her. He used murder to cover up his dirty deed, and he lived in that sin for apparently most of a year before he repented and turned to God's forgiveness.

One day a young man came to Jesus and asked life's most important question: What must I do to be saved? Jesus pointed him to some of the commandments: do not murder, commit adultery, steal, lie; but love your neighbor as yourself. With these words Jesus was not directing him to heaven. He wanted to lead him to a knowledge of his sin. But the man was looking for something he could do beyond obeying the commonly known Ten Commandments. He even claimed that he had kept them. But Jesus exposed him for what he was when he said: "'If you want to be perfect, go, sell your possessions and give to the poor, and you will have treasure in heaven. . . .' When the young man heard this, he went away sad, because he had great wealth" (Matthew 19:21,22). The poor rich man was a slave to his greedy heart.

The examples given above should cause us to do a little soul-searching. The man with a roving eye for beautiful women may be flirting (if he has not already succumbed) with a heart filled with lust. If we are constantly worrying about money matters, materialism may easily begin to dominate our life, and as a result we will not be satisfied, no matter how much we have.

The world is filled with people who think they are as free as birds, only to be slaves of some particular sin. What they need to hear is God's call to repentance and the message that proclaims freedom from sin.

Christ frees sinners

But how can one be free from the power of sin? Christ not only gives the answer; he is the answer. "To the Jews who had believed him, Jesus said, 'If you hold to my teaching, you are really my disciples. Then you will know the truth, and the truth will set you free.' They answered him, 'We are Abraham's descendants and have never been slaves of anyone. How can you say that we shall be set free?' Jesus replied, 'I tell you the truth, everyone who sins is a slave to sin. Now a slave has no permanent place in the family, but a son belongs to it forever. So if the Son sets you free, you will be free indeed'" (John 8:31-36).

Only those who hold to Jesus' teaching will know the truth and be his disciples. And what is the truth that sets us free from the power and consequences of sin? It is the blessed truth that Jesus himself summarized for Nicodemus. "God so loved the world that he gave his one and only Son, that whoever believes in him shall not perish but have eternal life" (John 3:16). It is the truth that God sent his eternal Son into the world, that he was born without sin, and that throughout his entire life he committed no sin. It is true that he was a man with feelings and that he endured the agony of being rejected by his own people. He suffered the humiliation and curse of the cross. But it is also true that he loved us so dearly that he shed his blood and gave his life, and even suffered hell itself when he was forsaken by God. Why? To redeem us from sin and from the power it would otherwise have over us. The Son has set us free; we are free indeed.

But what about the curse that God threatens to impose on all those who break his commandments? It's gone too. "Christ redeemed us from the curse of the law by becoming a curse for us, for it is written: 'Cursed is everyone who is hung on a tree'" (Galatians 3:13). God damned his own Son in order to save us *from* hellfire and *for* heaven's glory. Christ alone has freed us from sin's curse.

Many carry with them a heavy load of guilt. It may be one terrible incident in their life, or it may be the lifestyle they are leading. They are so deep into their sin they don't know how to get out. The only one who can free them from the guilt and bondage of their sin is Christ. What they need more than anything else is his word of forgiveness. That alone will remove their guilt, free them from a bad conscience, and move them to lead a godly life.

Jesus set Zacchaeus free. He was a wealthy man, and at least some of his wealth, by his own admission, was gotten dishonestly. When Jesus was passing through his town, Zacchaeus went to see him. Because he was a short man, he climbed up a tree to get a glimpse of this man, about whom he had heard so much. Jesus saw him and invited himself into his home. Jesus called him to faith, and by that encounter Zacchaeus was freed from the hold that money had had over him. That was evident from his resolve, "Here and now I give half of my possessions to the poor, and if I have cheated anybody out of anything, I will pay back four times the amount." Jesus left no doubt that this man had a complete change of heart when he said, "Today salvation has come to this house" (Luke 19:8,9). Zacchaeus was not coerced into taking such action. He did it freely because he had been freed by Christ from the slavery of his sin.

On one of his travels Jesus met an unsavory character at Jacob's well, a woman who had a bad reputation (John 4). She had never met Jesus before and was amazed at how much he knew about her. She had had five husbands and had discarded all of them, and the man she was living with when she met Jesus wasn't even her husband. But Jesus' word of grace and salvation freed her from the power her sinful nature had over her. Later, her witness to the people back in the town made that clear. "Come, see a man who told me everything I ever did. Could this be the Christ?" (John 4:29). She did not doubt that Christ had forgiven and freed her from her sin.

John Newton knew from personal experience what it meant to be freed by Christ from the slavery of sin. He was born in London in 1725. His father was a sea captain, and his mother was a devout Christian woman. She taught her son the truths of the Bible summarized in her catechism. When he was seven years old, his mother died. When he was seventeen, he joined his father at sea. By his own admission, he lived an ungodly life. One can well imagine what this young man did whenever his ship got into port. Only after he spent some time in the brig did he begin reading the Bible. Later, he was a sailor on a ship whose captain was a Christian. The captain instructed Newton in the truths of sin and salvation, and the Word of God he learned from this man converted him. The truth had made John Newton free.

He studied for the ministry and became a well-known preacher throughout England. He never forgot the abundance of love that his Lord had showered upon him. He knew what it meant to be graciously forgiven of all his sins and freed from their curse and power. John Newton wrote many hymns, including the following:

Amazing grace—how sweet the sound—
That saved a wretch like me!
I once was lost but now am found,
Was blind but now I see. (*Christian Worship* [CW] 379:1)

The Christian's dual nature

You may still be puzzled by the expression "freedom from sin." You know only too well that even though you believe in Christ, sin is an everyday companion. The Bible teaches two truths: Through Christ we are freed *from* sin, but we are not free *of* sin. At one and the same time, we are forgiven children of God and sinful human beings. How can that be? It is because, on this side of the grave, we will never be able to completely shed the sinful nature that we have inherited from our parents.

Our sinful nature is described in the Bible in a variety of ways: flesh, old Adam, old man, or old self. Paul confesses, "I know that nothing good lives in me, that is, in my sinful nature" (Romans 7:18). The apostle is saying that his old Adam was still just as evil as it was on the day he was born. Even after his conversion, it was still with him. And Jesus is describing how we all are by nature when he says, "From within, out of men's hearts, come evil thoughts, sexual immorality, theft, murder, adultery, greed, malice, deceit, lewdness, envy, slander, arrogance and folly" (Mark 7:21,22). Jesus makes it clear that disobedience begins in the heart, whether the deed is done or not. For example, the Bible tells us that hatred is as much a sin as murder (1 John 3:15) and that someone who lusts after a woman is guilty of adultery (Matthew 5:28).

God knew early in the history of the world that people's natures were corrupted by sin and that they would always have their sinful natures. "Every inclination of the thoughts of his [a person's] heart was only evil all the time" (Genesis 6:5). Our corrupted hearts don't stop being sinful the moment we are converted. Even though we have been freed from the guilt, the shame, the curse, and the power of sin, and we have been fully forgiven by God through Christ, we still have a sinful flesh clinging to us. Daily we must confess, "I know that nothing good lives in me, that is, in my sinful nature" (Romans 7:18). Before we came to faith in Christ, our old Adam was in complete control. We could do nothing that pleased God. Our hearts and lives were filled with sin.

But now for the good news. As Christians, we have another nature. We received it on the day we were converted. By the power of the Holy Spirit and by God's grace, we were brought to a knowledge of our sins, and we learned to trust in Christ as our Savior. We became new creatures. We now have a "new self, created to be like God in true righteousness and holiness" (Ephesians 4:24).

This new self is called by a number of different names: new man, inner being, spirit. The apostle Paul has described this new nature that God's Spirit has created in us. "Therefore, if anyone is in Christ, he is a new creation" (2 Corinthians 5:17).

Our old nature is only sinful; our new nature is only holy. Every Christian has this dual nature, and we believers have both natures. To put it another way, we are both saints and sinners at one and the same time.

The battle

The fact that we Christians have this dual nature explains what goes on in our hearts. A constant struggle is waging between our sinful nature and our new self. Why the warfare? "The sinful nature desires what is contrary to the Spirit, and the Spirit what is contrary to the sinful nature. They are in conflict with each other, so that you do not do what you want" (Galatians 5:17). Our old Adam says: Do the sin. You shouldn't deny yourself such pleasure. The new man replies: Sin is contrary to God's holy will; God wants you to live according to his Word. The one wants to indulge its sinful passions; the other fights sinful desires. The one lives for self; the other lives for God. That is the battle every Christian wages every day.

You may have asked yourself: Why is it so hard to be a Christian if God has brought me to faith and keeps me in it? Why do I still have to struggle so much to have pure thoughts, to speak the right words, to do the right thing? It is because we are Christians. If we didn't believe in Christ, there wouldn't be any spiritual wrestling at all. Our hearts and lives would be completely dominated by sin. But to follow Christ means to crucify our sinful flesh daily, for our old Adam does not die without a struggle.

Thus every day we confess our sins, repent of them, and turn to Jesus Christ as our one and only Savior. His grace is our strength to carry on our struggle with our sinful nature. This is one battle that will not be over until we die.

At one of our youth rallies, the presenter explained to the teens that they had this dual nature. They had been made new creatures through Christ, but they still had their old Adam with them, which was constantly trying to lead them into every kind of sin. He vividly demonstrated to the young people the battle they had to wage daily. With a movie projector, he showed an excerpt from a movie, depicting a sword fight. Using the white T-shirt he was wearing as a projection screen, he showed a battle between two swordsmen. And while they were watching it, the presenter reminded them of the fierce struggle they needed to wage against every kind of sin and temptation.

In the case of those who have been Christians for quite a few years, we know how easy it is for our sinful nature to get the upper hand. After all, it has happened in our lives often enough. For example, we are pleased to receive credit and praise for some accomplishment, but it is a struggle to receive it in such a way that gives all glory to God.

With all the lewdness depicted in magazines, movies, and TV, it is a struggle to lead a pure and decent life. Only too easily can lust dominate the sinful heart.

No generation has been as blessed with material possessions as we are today, but material things can easily become a distraction. Even worse, we know that materialism can easily take over our hearts and control our lives. We have a constant battle on our hands keeping Christ as our dearest treasure.

The two natures described above also explain the difference between the believer and the unbeliever. The ungodly person deals only with his sinful nature, for it completely controls his every thought, word, and deed. The unbeliever simply doesn't experience the spiritual conflicts that we have.

But we who call Jesus our Lord are God's new creation. Our faith in Christ is the dominating force in our lives. For us, the new man has the upper hand. Christ and his Word are in charge of our lives, and it has been that way since the day of our conversion. Our baptism helps in our struggle to lead Christian lives day after day.

In explaining the meaning of baptism for our daily life, Dr. Martin Luther wrote the following in his Small Catechism:

What does baptizing with water mean?

Baptism means that the old Adam in us should be drowned by daily contrition and repentance, and that all its evil deeds and desires be put to death. It also means that a new person should daily arise to live before God in righteousness and purity forever.

Where is this written?

Saint Paul says in Romans, chapter 6, "We were . . . buried with [Christ] through baptism into death in order that, just as Christ was raised from the dead through the glory of the Father, we too may live a new life."

We are living that new life in Christ now because he has freed us from sin.

5

Freedom from Death

All of us have seen death. We have not experienced it ourselves, but we have had a loved one who has died. For some it has left a void that can never be completely filled. But for all of us the funeral parlor makes us pause and think of our own mortality.

It should also direct our attention to the cause of death. More importantly, a loved one's departure from this life should prompt us to turn to him who is the source of all life—our God. And the truth of who God is and what he has to say to us about death is revealed in the Holy Scriptures.

Beginning of life

When God created heaven and earth, he made it in such a way that death had no part in it. When God created man, he created him to live, not merely for a certain number of years but forever in perfect harmony and communion with his Creator. Our God never does something that does not turn out well; rather, what he accomplishes is perfect in every sense of the word. He had a grand and glorious plan for the world he had created and for its people.

The crowning achievement of creation was man. He was made in the image of God, holy and righteous. The moment he was created he knew the true God, and he knew his holy will. Such knowledge was an integral part of his being.

God gave Adam and Eve the Garden of Eden as their home. He provided them with everything they needed for body and life. He told them they could eat the fruit of all the trees in the garden except one—the tree of the knowledge of good and evil. "When you eat of it," he warned, "you will surely die" (Genesis 2:17). With this special command, he was not burdening them with some grievous instruction. Rather, he was giving them a special way to demonstrate their love and devotion for him. God invited them to show their love for him who had made them and who gave them everything they needed to make living a joyful experience.

Origin of death

But early in the world's history, sin changed everything. Yes, everything. "We know that the *whole creation* has been groaning as in the pains of childbirth right up to the present time" (Romans 8:22). Every natural disaster finds its origin in what happened in the Garden of Eden. Those who had been holy were now sinful; those who had delighted in their Lord were now afraid of him. The holy image of God in which they had been created was totally lost. The life they had was gone; no longer would they keep on living. The day they ate of the forbidden fruit they began to die.

Sin would now corrupt the whole human race. And sin's constant companion would ever be death, for "sin entered the world through one man, and death through sin" (Romans 5:12). That is why we have been born to die. No exceptions exist—not even God's own Son, even though he did not deserve to die as we deserve.

Yes, we deserve to die. Because our life is filled with sin, we have earned death. For the Bible clearly teaches, "The wages of sin is death" (Romans 6:23).

Death and hell

Death is not simply the passing out of existence. Death by itself does not take us from one life to another that is a little better than the one we have now. We deserve the same fate that God gave to his rebellious angels. Jesus called it "eternal punishment" (Matthew 25:46) and "the eternal fire prepared for the devil and his angels" (Matthew 25:41). In other words, we deserve a death that will hurl us into eternal damnation.

Originally, hell was "prepared for the devil and his angels" (Matthew 25:41). They were the first to sin. And they have been "bound with everlasting chains for judgment on the great Day" (Jude 6).

Hell is described in Scripture as a place of eternal pain and suffering and torment, not even comparable to the most excruciating agony we have to endure in this life. The damned will be "thrown into the lake of fire" (Revelation 20:15). The rich man in hell is described as being in such torment that he pleaded with Abraham to send Lazarus to dip the tip of his finger in water and cool his

tongue because he was in such agony in the fire of hell
(Luke 16:19-31).

A little child was burned by a drop of grease. Her crying
indicated how much it hurt. Cold water relieved her pain,
and in an hour she had forgotten about it. But there will be
no relief for those who are being burned in hell. In fact,
God says excruciating pain will be their lot for eternity.
Christ described the anguish of a person in hell when he
cried on the cross, "My God, my God, why have you forsaken me?" (Matthew 27:46). During those hours on the
cross, Christ experienced the agony of the damned. He was
completely separated from the loving presence of his
Father. This, too, should be our lot. Christ, however, suffered the terrible agony of hell in our place. We no longer
need to fear God forsaking us or the anguish of the damned
that our death would otherwise have brought us.

Fear of death

And yet fears are all too often part of our lives. Think of
all the things you have been afraid of—losing a loved one,
getting sick, losing your job and not having enough money
to make ends meet, and too many other fears to mention.
But Jesus says that it is more valid to "be afraid of the One
who can destroy both soul and body in hell" (Matthew
10:28) than to be afraid of people who threaten to kill us
when we confess him openly. God is the only one who is
able to damn sinners. And if we don't believe in him, we
should be afraid of him.

But isn't fear natural? Isn't everyone afraid to die?
Because we are still sinners, fear remains a part of our lives.
When we are young, we are too busy living to give much
thought to dying. And when we are older, we are tempted
to put death out of our minds until we face some life-

threatening illness. But regardless of our age, we should regularly give serious thought to the end of our life. After all, death could happen to any one of us at any moment.

Christ and death

Thoughts of our dying need not be morbid reflections on where we are going and what will happen to those whom we leave behind. Rather, when we ponder death, we should focus on him who knows all about death and listen to what he has to say. We need to turn to the Bible repeatedly and read what God tells us about death and life after death.

While it is true that "by the trespass of the one man, death reigned through that one man," it is also true that "those who receive God's abundant provision of grace and of the gift of righteousness reign in life through the one man, Jesus Christ" (Romans 5:17). Adam brought death; Christ brings life.

But to bring us life Jesus had to die. His death, however, was not caused by his own sin. He was conceived by the Holy Spirit and born of a virgin mother. Joseph was not his flesh and blood father. Jesus, therefore, was not conceived and born in sin as we are. The gospels tell the story of a person who never spoke an unkind word, who was never guilty of any misdeed, and who could read the evil thoughts of other people but had no wicked thoughts of his own. He willingly led the life we could not lead—perfect in every way. He willingly carried our sins in his own body to the cross. And there he felt the full fury of God's wrath against all sins and suffered the agony of hell itself when he was separated from his Father. He died the death of the damned in our place. And he died of his own free will in accordance with God's plan of salvation.

What love our heavenly Father has for us! He gave him who was closest to his heart, his one and only beloved Son, into death for us! What love the Son had for us that he patiently and willingly bore the cross only he could bear, and died the death only he could die, thinking only of us all the time! "Greater love has no one than this, that he lay down his life for his friends. You are my friends if you do what I command" (John 15:13,14).[5] No greater love will the world ever see than the love that God has revealed to us in Christ.

Christ and life

He is risen! These three words proclaim to us that Jesus did everything his Father wanted him to do for our redemption. They also tell us that our freedom has been secured. We are not only freed from sin but also from sin's consequences—eternal death and hell, where temporal death would have otherwise taken us.

Christ's resurrection is the cornerstone of our Christian faith, for "if Christ has not been raised, your faith is futile; you are still in your sins" (1 Corinthians 15:17). And yet, the doctrine of the resurrection is under attack as never before. All kinds of theories are suggested in an attempt to explain away the bodily resurrection of Christ: Jesus was not really dead in the first place; the disciples only imagined that they saw Jesus alive; Jesus experienced a spiritual, not a bodily, resurrection. Such errors are no different from those of the Sadducees of Jesus' day. This sect denied that there would ever be a resurrection of the dead. Not surprisingly, the Sadducees were some of the most bitter opponents of Jesus.

Without Christ's resurrection, however, we would be left hopeless; we would have no confident hope of a glorious life after death. But the God-inspired writers of the gospels give us clear testimony that Jesus truly rose from the dead. And the apostle Paul confidently wrote to those in Corinth who were tempted to deny the resurrection: "But Christ has indeed been raised from the dead, the firstfruits of those who have fallen asleep" (1 Corinthians 15:20). We cannot conquer death and the grave, but Christ has done this for us. He had the power to lay down his life; he had the power to take it up again, and he exercised those powers. Now he wants us to remember his promise: "Because I live, you also will live" (John 14:19). He alone has freed us from death and its terror.

Our freedom from death

But can we really say that we have freedom from death? If judgment day does not precede our death, aren't we all going to die? Yes, we will die. But Jesus Christ and his redeeming work, confirmed by his resurrection from the dead, have given us an entirely new outlook on life and death. When Jesus came to Mary and Martha after their brother Lazarus had died, Jesus assured them that their brother would rise again. Then Martha made a beautiful confession about the resurrection that would take place on the Last Day. Jesus, of course, knew that there would be a resurrection at the end of the world. But he also knew that he was about to bring Lazarus back to life. Jesus spoke the following words to comfort the mourners of that day and also to reassure our faith when we experience the loss of a Christian loved one. "I am the resurrection and the life. He who believes in me will live, even though he dies; and whoever lives and believes in me will never die" (John 11:25,26).

Notice how Jesus directs our attention to himself, the I AM. He is not merely one who has been given the authority to raise someone from the dead. He already has the power to do it; it is in his very being. He is resurrection and life personified. He is the antithesis of the Grim Reaper.

First Jesus promises: "He who believes in me will live, even though he dies." He focuses our attention on himself as Savior, as the only one who will give life to the dead. If the deceased has died trusting in Jesus and confessing him to be his or her only hope of salvation, that individual will live a life that he or she has never had before, a life without sin and sorrow, without pain and the fear of death.

But then Jesus makes an even more startling promise: "Whoever lives and believes in me will never die." This applies to all of us who read these words and believe in Christ. Does he mean that we will never experience death even as Elijah and Enoch never did? Hardly. Death will merely transfer us from one life to another. The hymn writer states it this way: "And the grave that shuts us in shall but prove the gate to heaven" (CW 452:3). We have a bright future ahead of us.

Furthermore, the eternal life that Jesus promises us is already ours, and we will come into full enjoyment of it only when we die. For through Christ "death has been swallowed up in victory" (1 Corinthians 15:54). Christ has broken the chains of the grave, has released death's grim hold on us, and has given us life. Trusting in Christ's resurrection and his promises gives us the confidence that we have been freed from death.

Our eternal life

It is still true that when we die our bodies will return to the dust of the earth. In seemingly no time at all, our souls will be joined with our bodies at the resurrection of all the dead. Paradoxically, it will be the same body, and it won't be the same body. In eternity we will possess the same body we have now, only it will be transformed to be like Christ's glorious body—a body without sin and all its corruption (Philippians 3:21). Even if we have been blind all of our life, we will see God in all of his glory, face to face. And we will be glorified in our bodies even as Christ's body is glorified.

At one time or another all of us have wondered what heaven will really be like. Jesus gave us a foretaste of heaven when he was transfigured shortly before his death. His brilliance blinded his disciples. We will be reflections of his glory; our bodies too will be glorified. "When Christ, who is your life, appears, then you also will appear with him in glory" (Colossians 3:4).

The Bible also tells us that in heaven there will be "a Sabbath-rest for the people of God; for anyone who enters God's rest also rests from his own work, just as God did from his" (Hebrews 4:9,10). No more sweat and toil; only an eternal rest awaits us, a perfect rest for body and soul. We are able to say with David, "You [God] will fill me with joy in your presence, with eternal pleasures at your right hand" (Psalm 16:11). David is not speaking of the fleeting joys of this life but of a lasting joy in the presence of our Lord.

Such joy will never be marred, for John's vision reassures us: "He will wipe every tear from their eyes. There will be no more death or mourning or crying or pain, for the old order of things has passed away" (Revelation 21:4). No more death either for us or our loved ones who died in the Lord. In heaven we will come to the full and perfect realization of what Jesus meant when he assured us, "I am the resurrection and the life."

The end of this life

Have you ever wondered what the end of your life will be like? Will it be over in an instant? It may. That's why Jesus has told us always to be prepared for our final hour. Will we have to endure a slow and painful death, thinking that it could come at any time, even pleading that the Lord take us? In his wisdom and love he may delay that day, teaching us patience and increasing our longing to be with him in the heavenly home Christ has prepared for us by his redeeming work.

The Bible tells us how bravely some of God's saints died. John the Baptist was beheaded because of his faithful witness against the sins of Herod and because Herod refused to renege on a sinful oath (Matthew 14:1-12). Stephen was stoned to death because he unflinchingly proclaimed Christ's death and resurrection. But before he died, he prayed that God would forgive his enemies, and he commended his spirit to Jesus (Acts 7:54-60).

Will we be so brave? That really is the wrong question. Will we be trusting in Jesus Christ as our Savior when we breathe our last? is a better query. Saints of any era will confess their own weakness and God's faithfulness. Seminary professor Siegbert Becker was an outstanding theologian who had Luther's gift of putting profound doctrine in terms that laypeople could easily understand. When he learned that he had terminal cancer and had not long to live, he confessed, "I am not afraid of death; but I am afraid of dying." When he would die, he knew that he would have peace and joy forever with the Lord. But he readily acknowledged that he was still a sinner who had some fears, fears that would not completely leave him until the Lord would call him home.

What should our attitude be as we grow older and more infirm? Should we want to cling to life as long as we can? That is certainly a most natural feeling. In fact, if someone were to ask us today if we would like to continue living, we might hesitate. We might even be afraid of giving an answer unbecoming a Christian. But the apostle Paul expresses the proper outlook for any Christian when he writes, "For to me, to live is Christ and to die is gain" (Philippians 1:21).

Jesus Christ is the center of every Christian's life. He alone has the words of eternal life; he alone is life itself. Whatever situation we find ourselves in, we want nothing more than to glorify him who has saved us. That is living for Christ and not for self.

While our loved ones will feel a loss when we die, we will have gained a life that is beyond our human comprehension and experience. We may feel that we now have a good life. Each day we thank God for all the temporal and spiritual blessings he has showered on us. And yet we know there is a much better life awaiting us; and when we die, we will have gained it, for to "be with Christ . . . is better by far" (Philippians 1:23).

To the list of freedoms we have through Christ we add freedom from death. To have such freedom is real living.

6

Freedom from Satan

Satan was not always evil. But he has been in existence almost as long as the world. In order to find the origin of Satan, we must go back to the creation of the world.

Creation of angels

In the first chapter of Genesis, God has given us a record of how all things in the world came into existence. While other parts of the Bible tell us that there are angels, it does not tell us when they came into existence. We do know, however, that God created all things in heaven and on earth in six normal days. We also know that the angels are not little gods who are eternal, but that they are creatures of God. "For by him all things were created: things in heaven and on earth, visible and invisible . . . ; all things were created by him and for him" (Colossians 1:16). Angels are in heaven, and they are invisible.

From the Scriptures we know other things about angels. The word *angel* means messenger, and that is how God at times used them. Angels, for example, came to Lot and his family to warn them about the destruction of Sodom and Gomorrah (Genesis 19). Angels announced the birth of Christ to the shepherds (Luke 2). Angels were at the empty tomb to proclaim: "He has risen" (Matthew 28; Luke 24).

Characteristics of angels

Even though God would at times give them human forms, angels are spirits. They have no bodies. "Are not all angels ministering spirits . . . ?" (Hebrews 1:14). They have different personalities and a great deal of intellect. They willingly serve their Creator. They are called the "mighty ones who do his [God's] bidding, who obey his word" (Psalm 103:20). While God endowed them with great power, they are nevertheless limited in their power. They are not omnipresent as God is. And their number was fixed at their creation, for Jesus explained that God had not created them for marriage and procreation (Matthew 22:30). And all of them were created holy.

Origin of Satan

There are certain things we do not know about the angels. We do not know exactly when they were created, but we know it must have been on one of the six days of that first week. We do not know how many were created, but there must have been a great number, for the Bible refers to them as a host. Satan and the devils came from this large group of angels.

Since God created all of the angels with a free will, they could obey or disobey him. Some of the angels chose disobedience with Satan as their leader. We do not know what their original sin was. We are only told that "the angels . . . did not keep their positions of authority but abandoned their own home" (Jude 6) and they did this of their own free will.

While the fallen angels certainly lost their holiness, they did not lose many of the other characteristics they had possessed as angels. They are still spirits today, and they do have extraordinary powers.

Fate of Satan

God did not give these reprobates a second chance. He reserved judgment for them and made a special place for them—hell. "These [the devils] he has kept in darkness, bound with everlasting chains for judgment on the great Day" (Jude 6). This can hardly mean that God chained them in such a way that they no longer possessed any power, for the Bible pictures Satan as a roaring lion prowling about, looking for those whom he can bring into his kingdom (1 Peter 5:8).

Since the moment that Satan and his cohorts rebelled against God, they have had only one object in mind—to bring all mankind to the same fate that awaits them. When Satan came to Eve, he did not come as a messenger sent by God. He came as the father of lies and a murderer. He tempted Eve to desire the fruit God had forbidden her to eat and thereby brought sin and death into the world. He attacked the Seed of the woman whom God had promised would crush the head of the serpent, thus destroying Satan's power and his hold over mankind. He tempted Christ in the wilderness at the beginning of his ministry and marshaled all of his evil forces to try to destroy him at the end of his earthly mission. Satan has always had only one focus—to separate people from the true and living God. Yes, "the devil has been sinning from the beginning" (1 John 3:8) and wants all of us to do the same.

Allies of Satan

Satan has two major allies who help him carry out his evil deeds—the ungodly world and our sinful flesh.

We have mentioned that there is more than one evil angel. Repeatedly the Bible speaks of demons as if there is a host of them. They are all over the world doing Satan's bidding.

Most of the world is under his control. The unbelievers in the world serve only one master, Satan, even though most of them would vehemently deny it. Paul reminded the Ephesians that before their conversion to Christianity they "followed the ways of this world and of the ruler of the kingdom of the air, the spirit who is now at work in those who are disobedient" (Ephesians 2:2). "The ruler of the kingdom . . . the spirit" is Satan, and he has under his control all who are disobedient. That does not refer only to those who lead outwardly wicked lives. The devil works in the hearts and directs the lives of all those who do not believe in Christ. They do Satan's bidding. He forms a partnership with unbelievers to oppose Christians and to lead them into sin and unbelief. Observe how we and our children are constantly confronted with the allurements, the pleasures, the faulty reasoning of the worldly wise. Hence the warning: "Do not love the world or anything in the world. If anyone loves the world, the love of the Father is not in him" (1 John 2:15).

In addition to the ungodly world, we have in the fiber of our very being an enemy of God and a friend of Satan—the old Adam, our sinful flesh. Our sinful nature is our constant companion. Jesus was describing our sinful hearts when he said, "For from within, out of men's hearts, come evil thoughts, sexual immorality, theft, murder, adultery, greed, malice, deceit, lewdness, envy, slander, arrogance and folly" (Mark 7:21,22). Sin has so corrupted our hearts that every kind of wicked thought, word, and deed can flow from it. Do you wonder at times why you sinned? Temptation comes to us not only from without, from Satan and the sinful world, but also from within, from our inner being that has not completely shed its sinful nature. Paul had to confess that in spite of his calling to be a Christian and Christ's apostle, his sinful flesh still lived in him. "I know that nothing good lives in me, that is, in my sinful nature" (Romans 7:18).

Slaves of Satan

By nature we are not children of God who serve him, but we are slaves of Satan. "He who does what is sinful is of the devil, because the devil has been sinning from the beginning" (1 John 3:8). The apostle is not describing only unbelievers but also the natural state of every person born into this world. We are born in sin; we live in sin; we are servants of Satan by nature.

When the Jews boasted that Abraham was their father and that they had never been slaves of anyone, Jesus told them, "You belong to your father, the devil, and you want to carry out your father's desire. He was a murderer from the beginning, not holding to the truth, for there is no truth in him. When he lies, he speaks his native language, for he is a liar and the father of lies" (John 8:44). Jesus not only describes the devil and his ways, but he also instructs us that those who are without faith in Christ do not have God as their Father. In fact, their father is Satan himself. They listen to him and obey only his word. Jesus is describing the unbelieving world, and he is also telling us about our sad condition if we do not believe in him.

Satan's conqueror

We cannot take on Satan by ourselves and win. He will beat us every time. For when we were born into the world, we not only had a physical father but also a spiritual one, and he was Satan. We have not escaped his clutches on our own. Our gracious God knew that we could not escape Satan's power. He knew our hopeless and helpless condition from the beginning. That is why he promised to send the Savior who would crush the head of the serpent. "The reason the Son of God appeared was to destroy the devil's work" (1 John 3:8).

The Son of God was born into this world without sin, and he was a true human being with all of our weaknesses. He experienced hunger and thirst. He felt sorrow and the hatred of his enemies. He had emotions like ours, and he felt the assaults of Satan, especially when he was tempted in the wilderness and throughout his passion. But unlike the first Adam, he did not sin. He lived the only perfect life that has ever been lived on earth, and he did it because we haven't kept any command of God and because he was sent into this world to save us. He suffered and died innocently. He was not only innocent of the sins of which the Jews accused him, but he was innocent of *any* sin. Throughout his earthly life he was battling Satan and winning by not sinning. He lived and died for us. "He too shared in their [our] humanity so that by his death he might destroy him who holds the power of death—that is, the devil—and free those who all their lives were held in slavery by their fear of death" (Hebrews 2:14,15).

Christ Jesus came to free us from the stranglehold Satan had on us. He came as a human being. He lived as a human being. He was tempted as a human being. He died as a human being. He did the will of his Father as a human being. And he thereby destroyed the power of Satan.

Christ's victory is ours

Even though Christ has earned freedom from Satan's power for all people, all people are not free from his control. Christ's victory over Satan becomes ours only through faith in him. The moment we believed in Christ, Satan had no more claim over us; he could no longer completely control our lives. "Whoever believes and is baptized will be saved" (Mark 16:16) is not just a promise for the future. We are freed from Satan's complete control over us as soon as we come to faith and as long as we live believing in Christ as our one and only Savior.

Satan's attacks

But this does not mean that Satan and the other evil angels are not seeking us out. Quite the contrary. For our "enemy the devil prowls around like a roaring lion looking for someone to devour" (1 Peter 5:8). He is working day and night to bring us into his abominable kingdom.

Satan's primary objective is to destroy our trust in the true and living God. He knows that it is God's grace and the power of his Word that brought us to faith. He knows that it is only the gospel that keeps us in the true faith. And he also knows that true faith in God comes through hearing his Word. Separate a Christian from the Word of truth and you have separated him from his God and brought him into Satan's kingdom. And so he tempts us to reason: "It's not important that I attend church every time there is a service. I have some important things to take care of. I need the rest and relaxation. I can say a few prayers on my own that will be just as good." Once we start skipping church services, the devil will work overtime to keep us from hearing God's Word. And once we begin the backsliding, we are on the way to unbelief and hell. There is no nice way to describe what can so easily happen to any one of us.

And Satan knows our weak spots, which might include materialism. We may have good jobs, the best foods, comfortable homes, fine cars, and almost anything that hard work and some saving can bring us. We may take all of these things for granted and even be tempted to imagine that we deserve them. More and more we can easily forget that every good and perfect gift comes from our merciful God and that he is able to give all these things to us today and take them away tomorrow. If we would be impoverished tomorrow, are we prepared to say with Job: "The LORD gave and the LORD has taken away; may the name of the LORD be praised" (Job 1:21)?

The story of Job is worth considering as we learn about Satan and his diabolical ways. Job was one of the richest men of his day, but he was a man who did not live for his wealth. The Lord was his dearest treasure. One day the Lord confronted Satan: "Have you considered my servant Job? There is no one on earth like him; he is blameless and upright, a man who fears God and shuns evil" (Job 1:8). Job was righteous in the sight of God through faith in the promised Redeemer. To paraphrase Satan's reply to God, "Sure, Job believes in you and loves you. You have given him everything. Take it away and he will curse you." Then the Lord allowed Satan to take away everything Job had, even his children—everything, that is, except Job's life. And what was Job's response? He praised God. What would be our response if a similar disaster struck? By grace our response would prove that our God-given faith has truly overcome the world and its prince, Satan.

Another weakness may be a strong sexual desire. Originally every sexual desire was holy. Our first parents were so innocent they walked around naked without any shame. But the sin they brought into the world corrupted their hearts and ours with sinful desires. And even though we have found forgiveness for such sins in Jesus, lust can easily still plague us. Today we have the visuals in magazines, on TV, and in the movies that are intended, yes, by Satan, to arouse lust in our hearts. The way someone dresses may arouse us. Or it may be the way another looks at us. All of these are Satan's tools to lead us into sin and keep us there.

Hatred can easily get the best of us. Some people's personalities might turn us off. Or people may treat us "like dirt" and in many little ways let us know that they don't like us. They may do us some terrible wrong, so that we are tempted to say in our hearts (with Satan himself whispering in our ear): "I will never forgive them for what they have done to me." In the Lord's Prayer we are asking God to forgive our sins because of what Christ has done for us, and we are moved by such love flowing daily from our God to forgive those who sin against us. Jesus reminds us there is no end to God's forgiveness; neither should we place a limit on the number of times we forgive others their sins against us (Matthew 18:21-35).

Satan also wants to lead us into false belief. He wants us to do what he convinced Eve to do, namely, to doubt

God's Word. He raises the same question he asked Eve in the Garden: "Did God really say?" When you are listening to a faithful preacher and teacher of God's Word, Satan wants you to challenge every truth you hear, especially those that are beyond your reason. Is God really triune? Am I really saved without any good works on my part? Do you mean God wants man to be the head of the woman? Do you think that all religions don't worship the same God? Aren't there many paths to heaven? Is it really only possible to worship God and be saved through Jesus Christ? Satan knows that it takes only one seed of doubt to plant unbelief.

Satan will attack us where he knows we are most vulnerable. And he is relentless in his temptations. They come every moment of our lives, and they will not end until we die. Only then will we be free from his ferocious attacks.

Our defense

But what can we do in the meantime? How can we ward off the deadly arrows of temptation the devil is shooting at us? What kind of defense do we have?

Jesus showed us the way. When he was tempted in the wilderness by Satan as he was beginning his ministry, he employed a weapon that he has now placed into the hands of each of his followers—the Word of God. Three times the devil attacked, and each time Jesus thrust him back with the words: "It is written." Jesus was referring to what had been written in the Old Testament Scriptures. He overcame Satan's deception and lies with the Word of Truth. The father of lies cannot stand up against the truth. It beats him every time.

The apostle Paul also directs us to the weapons of our warfare when he writes in Ephesians 6:10-18:

Finally, be strong in the Lord and in his mighty power. Put on the full armor of God so that you can take your stand against the devil's schemes. For our struggle is not against flesh and blood, but against the rulers, against the authorities, against the powers of this dark world and against the spiritual forces of evil in the heavenly realms. Therefore put on the full armor of God, so that when the day of evil comes, you may be able to stand your ground, and after you have done everything, to stand. Stand firm then, with the belt of truth buckled around your waist, with the breastplate of righteousness in place, and with your feet fitted with the readiness that comes from the gospel of peace. In addition to all this, take up the shield of faith, with which you can extinguish all the flaming arrows of the evil one. Take the helmet of salvation and the sword of the Spirit, which is the word of God. And pray in the Spirit on all occasions with all kinds of prayers and requests. With this in mind, be alert and always keep on praying for all the saints.

The picture is that of an ancient warrior; however, our battle is not physical but spiritual. In any battle the proper weapons are necessary to insure victory. We need to use all of the armor God has placed at our disposal, so that we can take our "stand against the devil's schemes." Note the list: "the belt of truth"—Christ and his Word are the truth; "the breastplate of righteousness"—Christ's righteousness, a righteousness that is wholly acceptable to God, has become ours; "the gospel of peace"—peace with God is ours because God has freely forgiven our sin for Jesus' sake; "the shield of faith"—our trust in God and his promises protects us from the deadly arrows of sin and error; "the helmet of salvation"—this protection is ours as God's dear children and heirs of heaven; "the sword of the Spirit, which is the word of God"—this offensive weapon enables us to be "strong in the Lord," "to stand [our] ground," and to beat back Satan's attacks.

Be assured there is a word from our God in the Holy Scriptures for every one of Satan's temptations. When we are tempted to put too much stock in our worldly goods, the reminder comes: "Man does not live on bread alone, but on every word that comes from the mouth of God" (Matthew 4:4). When we are tempted to doubt God's love for us, the Word comes to strengthen us that nothing "will be able to separate us from the love of God that is in Christ Jesus our Lord" (Romans 8:39). When we are tempted to commit some sexual sin, Joseph's words to Potiphar's wife come to mind: "How . . . could I do such a wicked thing and sin against God?" (Genesis 39:9). When we are tempted to hold a grudge, we are reminded of all that Jesus has done for us so that our slate of sin is wiped clean. And that redeeming love of Christ is found throughout the Bible.

Some have wondered why we place so much emphasis on the Bible in our preaching and teaching, why we encourage our children to memorize pertinent Bible passages and to become lifelong Bible students. The answer is simple—to keep us in the true faith, for the Word that we can quickly recall will be our defense when we are suddenly face to face with one of Satan's temptations.

When I was confirmed, my parents gave me a leather-bound Bible. My father promised, "When you wear out this one, I will buy you another one." He knew what would keep me in the faith; and he knew better than I did then the many temptations I would face. He wanted me to have the Word of God in my heart and the sword of the Spirit always at hand.

To all of us this word of encouragement comes: "Submit yourselves, then, to God. Resist the devil, and he will flee from you" (James 4:7). Christ has secured our freedom from Satan by his redeeming work. Through faith in him we will not lose that freedom. Luther put it this way in his hymn "A Mighty Fortress Is Our God":

> Though devils all the world should fill,
> All eager to devour us,
> We tremble not, we fear no ill;
> They shall not overpow'r us.
> This world's prince may still
> Scowl fierce as he will,
> He can harm us none.
> He's judged; the deed is done!
> One little word can fell him. (CW 201:3)

7

Freedom for Service

Service is important. Ask any successful businessman. Our own experiences with a variety of businesses tell us the same thing. We might get a good price, but if the service is bad, we will think twice before we go back to that store. Good service is worth a lot to us. I was reminded of that when my favorite chair broke. The mechanical part of it was still under warranty, so I called the store where I purchased it, and the person to whom I spoke stated that his store would fix it free of charge. I reminded him that the company that made the chair had a warranty on it. He replied, "Our store has a much better warranty than any manufacturer. We'll be happy to fix it for you." That's the kind of store I like to do business with. That's service.

88 CHRISTIAN FREEDOM

Called to serve

Jesus came to serve. On one occasion Jesus told his disciples: "I am among you as one who serves" (Luke 22:27). He served when he lived in obedience to his parents. He served when he went from town to town proclaiming his gospel of salvation. He served by providing food for people who were hungry. He served when he gave the blind sight and caused the deaf to hear. But what is most important, he served the whole human race when he laid down his life to remove the guilt of all sins. Jesus is serving us today as he pleads our case before the throne of our heavenly Father, asking God to forgive our sins. He is serving us by being with us at all times as he promised.

We too are called to serve. "Serve the Lord with fear" (Psalm 2:11), the psalmist encourages us. He is not speaking of the slavish kind of service that comes from fear of punishment. Rather, this fear accompanies faith, and that kind of fear has a high regard for the living God and his Word. While we are saved by faith alone, faith in Christ is never alone. Faith is always accompanied by loving service.

Eager to serve

If we have been called to serve, why then are we not always eager to serve our Lord? It's because our sluggish and sinful nature so often gets in the way. That is why the husband does not always serve his wife the way he should, nor the children their parents, nor the employee the employer.

In one of his Christmas sermons, Luther had this to say, "There are many of you in this congregation who think to yourselves: 'If only I had been there [in Bethlehem when Jesus was born]! How quick I would have been to help the baby! I would have washed his linen. How happy I would have been to go with the shepherds to see the Lord lying in the manger!' Yes, you would! You say that because you know how great Christ is, but if you had been there at that time, you would have done no better than the people of Bethlehem. . . . Why don't you do it now? You have Christ in your neighbor. You ought to serve him, for what you do for your neighbor in need you do to the Lord Christ himself."[6]

We can all use such admonishment and encouragement. At such times we need especially to recall God's grace in Christ. Christ's love for us makes us eager to serve him and our fellowman, and he wants ours to be a willing service.

Jesus encourages willing service when he invites all of his followers to take up their crosses and follow him. He has warned us that we will have to suffer this world's scorn and hatred because we confess our faith in him. But he also entreats us: "Come to me, all you who are weary and burdened, and I will give you rest. Take my yoke upon you and learn from me, for I am gentle and humble in heart, and you will find rest for your souls. For my yoke is easy and my burden is light" (Matthew 11:28-30). Jesus does not want us to struggle under the burden of law and sin. As far as our salvation is concerned, Christ has removed the demands and curses of the law. He has given rest for our souls by forgiving our sinful past. He wants us to know and feel that our service for him is "easy" and not a heavy burden.

Man-made rules for service

What kind of service are we talking about? We might be tempted to wait for some instruction from the church and do it simply because the church says it's the right thing to do. But if the leaders in the church are not thoroughly committed to the Word of God, we can easily be misled into doing service that is not pleasing to God.

For example, today the ecumenical movement has a great deal of appeal. By that we mean church leaders who do not take doctrinal differences seriously and instead promote a kind of unity with anyone who calls himself a Christian. They might say that there is no greater service we could do for God than to unite with other Christians. And we could easily reason that it does not matter with whom we worship, for we all honor the same God. In other words, it could seem right for us to participate in a fellowship that tolerates false teaching. But this is hardly the kind of activity God encourages when he warns us to beware of false prophets and to avoid those who cause divisions in the church by the errors they teach (Matthew 7:15; Romans 16:17). Such service is man-made and not God-directed.

Self-chosen works can easily lead to self-righteousness. The Pharisees of Jesus' day are good examples of what can happen to those who fail to heed the warning of God: "Do not add to what I command you" (Deuteronomy 4:2). They wanted to be on a little higher level than the run-of-the-mill Jew. So they tried to do more than what God had commanded in his law. In time their oral traditions and rules were placed on a par with God's law. Worse, they eventually considered their traditions more important than God's commandments. Jesus condemned such self-chosen service when he said to them, "You nullify the word of God for the sake of your tradition" (Matthew 15:6).

Over the years, the Roman Catholic Church has done the same thing. It holds that edicts of its church councils and the pope are as valid as anything written in the Bible.[7]

For example, it has set its own rules concerning marriage, divorce, and annulment.

The Mormons have also set up a complicated set of rules for those who join the Mormon church. For example, they have labeled the drinking of tea and coffee and alcoholic beverages a sin.[8]

We could cite many other churches that make up their own rules and regulations for their members to follow, as if such rules were God's will and command. In each case the church body places its members under its man-made laws. Its followers are led to believe that obeying the church's rules will make them right with God. Jesus condemns such churches when he says, "Their teachings are but rules taught by men" (Matthew 15:9). Christ has freed us from all such human regulations, as the apostle Paul shows us: "Since you died with Christ to the basic principles of this world, why, as though you still belonged to it, do you submit to its rules: 'Do not handle! Do not taste! Do not touch!'? These are all destined to perish with use, because they are based on human commands and teachings" (Colossians 2:20-22).

God's guidelines for service

It is no wonder, then, that many are easily confused about what kind of service is pleasing to God. While God does not spell out everything we should do in our Christian lives, he certainly has given us some important guidelines. We call a summary of these guidelines the Ten Commandments. From them we learn what kind of service is pleasing to God. Some examples follow.

We know how happy we are when our children respect us and all those whom God has placed over them. Such an attitude and obedience is pleasing to God. Children are performing an important service for God when they live in accordance with the Fourth Commandment.

As Jesus reminds us, the poor are always with us (Mark 14:7). We are serving them and our God whenever we are willing and able to relieve their physical needs. This is a vital part of obeying the Fifth Commandment.

We not only come together in our church services to hear the Word of God and to sing his praises, but we also glorify his name by witnessing to others about Jesus. The Second and Third Commandments guide us in such service. The more we read the Ten Commandments with Luther's Bible-based explanations in our catechism, the more we realize how much they are able to guide us in our everyday living. In his Word, God has declared us free so that we may live a life of service for him and our neighbor. And in that same Word, he gives us the guidelines for godly living.

We need these guidelines that God has given us in the Ten Commandments. Even though he has written his law into our hearts, we still cannot always distinguish right from wrong because we have a sinful nature. As a result, something that we may think is all right is all wrong. And even some things we might consider wrong may not be contrary to God's will.

A pastor who had returned to the parish ministry after many years of teaching in a synodical worker-training school was asked what he found different in the ministry in a congregation today. Without hesitation he replied, "Young people living together outside of marriage." Because the practice has become so widespread in the world, and even is considered simply another way of life by many, these young Christians did not think it was a sin against the Sixth Commandment. They had forgotten or did not want to remember what they had learned from the Bible concerning the leading of a "pure and decent life in words and actions." They were in great peril because they were abandoning the Christian faith and life.

We can make moral decisions too easily on the basis of our reason, instead of asking the question, "What does God's Word say?" For example, our communities have certain regulations, especially if we are planning to build. The building codes are there for our good, but in some cases they may seem unreasonable. Some of them could easily be ignored, and nobody would know the difference. Not to abide by the codes may seem to be a minor infraction, but it is still in violation of the laws of man and of God, who has instructed us to submit ourselves "to the governing authorities" (Romans 13:1).

The moral decay of the world is all around us. And the ungodly and the unbelieving do not care what the Bible says. The world is intent on doing as it pleases. And the worldly person's sinful lifestyle can easily begin to rub off on us. What we hear others saying tends to dull our consciences. For example, so much profanity is all around us that it may hardly bother us that such words are a sin against the Second Commandment. What at one time seemed to be disgraceful no longer shocks us. For that reason we need God's law, both as a mirror for our sins and as a guide for our living. Only then will our lives of service be pleasing to the God who has freed us.

Service in the church

What kind of service can we perform for our gracious Lord? Our faith in Christ has prompted us to seek others who share our faith. We join together in a congregation to worship and serve God. In the church we have pastors and teachers and missionaries who have dedicated themselves to full-time service to the Lord. But the church is made up of many members, all contributing to the well-being of Christ's kingdom. The congregation selects a variety of people to assume certain responsibilities—duties, if you will—that enable it to function efficiently. If you would list every person who is serving in some capacity in the church, you would probably be amazed at how many members are voluntarily dedicating hours of service to the Lord.

For example, the church council is usually made up of some of the most dedicated men in the congregation. They spend many hours of their time in meetings and assigned duties. The treasurer probably puts in as much time as anyone, yet his work goes largely unnoticed by most members. But he performs a valuable service to the congregation by paying the bills and reporting the financial status of the congregation.

As another example, the Sunday school teachers perform an important ministry in the congregation. Sunday after Sunday they instruct Christ's lambs in the saving truths of his Word. They spend many hours preparing their lessons and attending meetings so they can nourish the souls entrusted to their care.

In addition, ladies' groups may be devoted to some of the physical needs of the church. Again, most of us are unaware of all they are doing and perhaps take their services for granted. They are often just as dedicated as the women who were hurrying to Jesus' tomb early on Easter morning to care for the body of their Lord.

One of the most important and difficult tasks in the congregation is trying to reach the backsliders. They are people who are spiritually starving themselves to death. They rarely attend the worship services to hear the Word of God. They have despised the reception of the Lord's Supper for an extended period of time. And they desperately need admonition and encouragement. Very often when the pastor talks to them about their neglect of the means of grace, they will say, "Yes, I know, pastor. I will try to be there." And maybe they will be, for a time. But then many of them slide back into their bad habit of neglecting to hear God's Word. In such cases the elders play a vital role in assisting the pastor. They spend many an evening calling on delinquent members. Sometimes they are able to reach people with evangelical admonition when the pastor has had little success. Jesus said, "There is rejoicing in the presence of the angels of God over one sinner who repents" (Luke 15:10). Those who have been freed by Christ are God's instruments in freeing others from their sins.

Life of service

But we should not imagine that service to God is performed only by serving in some capacity in the church. God wants our entire life to be one of service. Luther reminds us in his explanation of the Second Article of the Apostles' Creed that Christ has redeemed us when we were lost and condemned, so that we may "live under him in his kingdom, and serve him in everlasting righteousness, innocence and blessedness."

As Christians we serve our Lord in the most ordinary ways: a person is faithful in his work for his employer, and an employer is considerate of his employees; a father carries out his responsibilities as a Christian parent, properly guiding and disciplining his children and showing love and consideration for his wife; a mother makes the meals, cleans the house, and washes the clothes. When Christians do all of these acts out of love for their Savior, they are truly serving God.

Motivation for service

Motivation has much to do with the kind of service we perform. Doing the right thing for the right reason pleases God. Doing what seems to be right for the wrong reason is sin. Cain and Abel are good examples of how important motivation is. Both offered sacrifices to God. Abel did this in faith, trusting in God's gracious promise of a Savior. "By faith Abel offered God a better sacrifice than Cain did. By faith he was commended as a righteous man, when God spoke well of his offerings. And by faith he still speaks, even though he is dead" (Hebrews 11:4). Abel's sacrifice expressed his love for God, who loved him. Cain's heart lacked faith; his heart was filled with hatred and jealousy. His sacrifices were unacceptable to God.

Why do we do what we do? Maybe we get personal satisfaction out of a job well done. Maybe we like to receive a pat on the back every now and then. Or it could be that we like the financial rewards that hard work brings. What we mentioned so far will not score points with God. So easily our actions can be selfish and self-serving. Therefore, we want to be certain that our motivations are God-pleasing.

The apostle Paul is speaking of the motivation that should characterize our Christian life when he writes, "Christ's love compels us" (2 Corinthians 5:14). No one has shown us greater love than Christ. No one gave us everything the way he did. With his words and redemptive deeds he has assured us of our eternal destiny. Through Christ we know who we are and where we are going. And today we know what we want to do—live a life of service for him. "He died for all, that those who live should no longer live for themselves but for him who died for them and was raised again" (2 Corinthians 5:15). Truly, Christ freed us for service.

God has not given his Son to be our Savior, and Christ has not laid down his life so that we can sit on our hands and do nothing. He has freed us from the demands of the law, from the punishment for sin, and from Satan's power in order to motivate and empower us. Now we want to serve him, and this God-given desire moves us to action. Christ's love for us makes ours a joyful service.

Motivation, like faith, is hidden in the recesses of the human heart. And only God knows for sure why people act the way they do.

For the glory of God

When Jesus encouraged us to let our "light shine before men, that they may see [our] good deeds and praise [our] Father in heaven" (Matthew 5:16), he was not speaking of some extraordinary service we should perform, but simple, everyday Christian living. That will be enough to cause others to praise our heavenly Father.

We should not do what we do for own glory. Self-glory is a product of the sinful flesh. But our purpose in life is that God and his grace be praised. That means even in the most ordinary things of life. "Whether you eat or drink or whatever you do, do it all for the glory of God" (1 Corinthians 10:31). When we are tempted to be proud of our accomplishments, the Bible reminds us, "It is God who works in you to will and to act according to his good purpose" (Philippians 2:13).

Sin has so permeated our being that nothing we do can be perfect, even when we consciously perform some service for God. The most faithful servants in Christ's church realize that they still have a sinful flesh that daily gives them trouble. We are able to identify with the words of Paul, "I have the desire to do what is good, but I cannot carry it out. For what I do is not the good I want to do; no, the evil I do not want to do—this I keep on doing" (Romans 7:18,19). Yes, it is a constant struggle with our sinful flesh to serve Christ faithfully. Even our best service to God is marred by sin.

How, then, can God accept any of our service? "It does not . . . depend on man's desire or effort, but on God's mercy" (Romans 9:16). By his grace God has called us to faith and to ministry. By his grace he keeps us in the faith and accepts our service. For when Christ cleansed us of all our sins, he enabled us to stand righteous in God's sight. No longer does God see our deeds of love as filled with imperfections. They have been sanctified, made holy by him whose name is holy, the Holy Spirit. Because of all that Christ has done, God no longer sees the blotches of sins on our service. In fact, our deeds of love are now so pure that they will accompany us into eternity. "Blessed are the dead who die in the Lord from now on. . . . they will rest from their labor, for their deeds will follow them" (Revelation 14:13).

8

Freedom in the Church

Some people would challenge that statement, "freedom in the church." "There is no freedom in a church," they say. They view the church as an institution that burdens people with all kinds of rules and regulations. In fact, some unbelievers would never join a church because they think in so doing they would lose their freedom. One teenager candidly told a missionary that he did not want to be instructed and baptized because then he would have to stop having sexual relations with his girlfriend.

The church
Before we discuss freedom in the church, we should have a clear understanding of what the church is according to the Scriptures. It is, of course, not a building,

although we often speak of the building in which we worship as our church. It is not in itself a congregation, although some members of a Christian congregation may be members of Christ's church. Nor is it, strictly speaking, the sum total of all the people belonging to churches that claim to be Christian.

The church, as the Bible defines it, is all those who believe in Jesus Christ as their Savior. On the first Pentecost "the Lord added to their number [to the church] daily those who were being saved" (Acts 2:47). While we will assume that all those who belong to our congregation are members of the Christian church, we do not know with absolute certainty who the believers are, for we cannot look into their hearts, where faith resides. "Man looks at the outward appearance, but the LORD looks at the heart" (1 Samuel 16:7). For that reason the true church of Christ is invisible. However, when we observe a person confessing the true Christian faith and living the Christian life, we assume that his words and actions are genuine.

The Word builds the church

Still, we know where the church is on earth. Jesus had given his disciples their marching orders when he commanded them, "Go into all the world and preach the good news to all creation" (Mark 16:15); "make disciples of all nations" (Matthew 28:19). For 2,000 years the followers of Christ have been spreading the Good News. Wherever the gospel of Jesus Christ is preached on earth, there his church will be found. For God has promised, "My word that goes out from my mouth . . . will not return to me empty, but will accomplish what I desire and achieve the purpose for which I sent it" (Isaiah 55:11). God desires that everyone come to a knowledge of the truth and be saved. His purpose in sending us out to preach the gospel is that sinners may hear God's Word, believe it, and be saved. God's purpose is achieved because wherever the gospel is preached, people will be converted. That's in keeping with his promise that his Word never returns empty.

The Word of our God is the focus of the church. We hear the Word preached; we have the Word taught to our children; we spread the Word in our community and throughout the world. And what is most important, God wants us to be faithful to his Word, neither adding to it nor subtracting from it. Jesus has promised, "If you hold to my teaching, you are really my disciples. Then you will know the truth, and the truth will set you free" (John 8:31,32). This freedom we have described in the previous chapters is a freedom that is based on the truth of God's Word.

By freedom in the church we do not mean that we can gather ourselves together, call ourselves Christians, and then do as we please. God has given us both his law and his gospel for our faith and our living. He has made it abundantly clear that his Word, and his Word alone, is to be taught in the church and obeyed.

Adiaphora

But there are many things we do in the church that are not prescribed in the Bible. These are called *adiaphora*. An adiaphoron (singular of adiaphora) is something that God neither commands nor forbids in the Bible. The apostle Paul is speaking of them when he writes, "Everything is permissible" (1 Corinthians 10:23). Again, the "everything" refers to those matters that God has not prescribed in his law to guide our actions.

For example, God has not told us at what time or on what day of the week we should hold church services. He has not told us to have monthly or quarterly congregational meetings or whether we must have them at all. While he has told us, "Feed my lambs," he has not instructed us how we should carry out this general command. All of the above are adiaphora.

What are some other adiaphora that enable us to exercise our Christian liberty? Let us use as examples some of the most common experiences we have in the church.

Throughout the year we have a variety of church services. We have at least one every Sunday, some during the week, some in the evening, some during the day. They usually last about an hour. Certainly a command on what days and what time to hold our services is not found in the Bible.

Ceremonial law

That has not always been the case among God's people. After God led the Israelites out of slavery in Egypt, Moses took them to Mt. Sinai. There God gave Moses his law, and Moses transmitted it to the people. Included in his many commandments were detailed instructions as to when they were to worship and what their priests were to do. For example, God told them that he wanted them to worship on the seventh day of the week, Saturday. He called it the Sabbath. That day was to be a day of rest, both for their bodies and their souls. The word *Sabbath* means rest.

For the Israelites the Sabbath law and all of the Old Testament ordinances pertaining to worship were constant reminders of the promised Messiah. Once Christ had come and fulfilled what the Scriptures had prophesied about him, God freed his people from these Old Testament ceremonial laws. The Bible informs us about the freedom that the New Testament church has. "Do not let anyone judge you by what you eat or drink, or with regard to a religious festival, a New Moon celebration or a Sabbath day. These are a shadow of the things that were to come; the reality, however, is found in Christ" (Colossians 2:16,17).

Since Christ has come, the purpose of these Old Testament laws has been fulfilled. No longer does God, for example, forbid his people to eat pork. And God has given us the liberty to choose the days and the times when we can come together to hear his Word. The early church exercised its Christian freedom and selected the first day of the week for its regular worship.

Our worship

Another example of the freedom we have through Christ is the way we worship God. Even though our liturgies are based on various portions of the Scriptures, God did not prescribe for us what order of church services we should conduct and when we should use them. That is why we have a variety of services and do not always follow the same liturgy in every church service. This may help us be more attentive to what we are hearing and saying in the church service, and thus the various services become more meaningful.

When false teachers were troubling the early church by insisting that the church must retain the Old Testament ceremonies, Paul wrote a letter to the congregations he had founded in Galatia. They were experiencing a serious doctrinal problem because the false teachers were robbing them of their Christian freedom by teaching that the law of God must be obeyed for salvation. These Christians were in great danger of losing their faith in Christ, who fulfilled the whole law of God for them. Then their faith would have been resting on their own works and not on God's grace. Paul wrote, "It is for freedom that Christ has set us free. Stand firm, then, and do not let yourselves be burdened again by a yoke of slavery" (Galatians 5:1).

Today we, who believe that we are saved alone by God's grace through faith in Christ, are enjoying the freedom that Christ has won for us by choosing the days of our worship and by using different kinds of liturgies in our church services.

Forms of ministry

The Old Testament church had a form of ministry that God had closely regulated. It was a ministry that was carried out by his prophets and priests. Today we do not have priests making regular sacrifices for us because the purpose of the Old Testament priesthood was fulfilled by Christ when he sacrificed himself for the sins of the world. But what has been retained and is still in place is the ministry of the Word of God. For the church to carry out the responsibility of preaching the gospel for the salvation of sinners, God "gave some to be apostles, some to be prophets, some to be evangelists, and some to be pastors and teachers" (Ephesians 4:11). Christ called some of these messengers directly, such as the apostles. Others he calls through his believers, as we often do in our congregational meetings.

While we know some of the things the early leaders in the church did in their various ministries, God has not given us a job description for their offices. Rather, he has given his New Testament church the freedom to form the kind of ministry that will best serve his church at various times and in a variety of circumstances. For example, even though teachers are mentioned as functioning in the early church, the Bible could not be referring to elementary school teachers such as we have in our church schools because there were no such schools in apostolic times, as far as we know.

Although the public office of the ministry was instituted by God, the outward forms of the ministry were not. Today we establish those forms of ministry that we believe will best serve the spiritual needs of God's people and the work of his church. Therefore, a variety of offices for ministry have been established in our congregations and our synod, such as pastors, Lutheran elementary school and high school teachers, Sunday school teachers, professors at our colleges and seminary, administrators, and many others.

Gifts to God

Another difference in the church before and after the time of Christ is the matter of our gifts to the Lord. In the Old Testament, God told the Israelites how much to give so that the priests and Levites could be supported. It was called a tithe, one-tenth of what they earned. Again, this is another of the ancient Jewish ordinances that God has abolished. Instead, we are free to bring to the Lord whatever gifts we choose as a fruit of our faith and for the advancement of his kingdom. The love that Christ has for us should move us to generous giving. "For you know the grace of our Lord Jesus Christ, that though he was rich, yet for your sakes he became poor, so that you through his poverty might become rich" (2 Corinthians 8:9). Christ became poor when he gave up everything for us, even his own life. Now we are rich in God's gracious forgiveness. In response to the love that Christ gave us, the Bible encourages "each man [to] give what he has decided in his heart to give, not reluctantly or under compulsion, for God loves a cheerful giver" (2 Corinthians 9:7).

Freedom not confusion

In granting us such liberties in the way the church may conduct its affairs, God is not encouraging everyone to do his own thing. That would only promote confusion and disorder in the church. For example, even though the command to preach the gospel is given to all Christians, everyone in the church is not called to proclaim the Word on Sunday morning. Rather, someone is called by God through the congregation for that special purpose. Imagine what would happen if a number of people would begin arguing about who would conduct the church service on a particular Sunday morning. Such behavior would be an abuse of our Christian liberty. The Scriptures offer us a general principle to follow: "Everything should be done in a fitting and orderly way" (1 Corinthians 14:40). Our church services should be orderly.

Brotherly love

Also, we should function as Christ's church with a loving concern for others. Brotherly love will discourage us from insisting that our way is the only way or even the best way when it comes to adiaphora. The exercise of our Christian liberty, rightly done, does not disrupt Christian unity but fosters it. For the Lord wants us to "make every effort to keep the unity of the Spirit through the bond of peace" (Ephesians 4:3).

Here is a practical example of how members can demonstrate their love for one another. A growing congregation perceives a need for its church facilities to be expanded. This congregation also supports a Lutheran elementary school that is bursting at the seams. The members ask, "Which building program should come first—the church or the school?" A committee is appointed to study the matter, and committee members make their findings known to the congregation along with their recommendation. The debate then begins. One group feels that since the church service is the center of all spiritual activities, the church building should be constructed first. Another group feels that the future of the congregation lies with the children; therefore, their Christian education should be the primary concern.

Who is right? Both are—for what they are debating is an adiaphoron. The decision is finally made by a majority vote. What a tragedy if that vote is allowed to cause a permanent rift in the congregation! Rather, the sentiment of one man in a similar meeting expressed Christian love: "I do not agree with the decision, but I will support it." For him, any breach that might occur should be avoided out of love for God and for his fellow members.

Also, if a congregation is trying to decide whether or not to start its own school, strong feelings might be expressed on both sides of the issue. But once the decision has been made, it should be the prayer of all the members that none would harbor ill feelings. Whatever we do in the church should be done in the spirit of Christian love to the glory of God.

Some might be tempted to test the limit in matters of adiaphora. They might ask the questions, "Where does the Bible say we should do this?" or "Where does the Bible say we are forbidden to do that?" In reality, they are asking, "How much is permitted?" But they are asking the wrong question. The foremost query should be, "What will best glorify God?" For our desire should be "that in all things

God may be praised through Jesus Christ. To him be the glory and the power for ever and ever" (1 Peter 4:11).

Freedom not to be abused

Even though some matters are neither commanded nor forbidden in the Bible, there are other things that Christians should consider. In the apostolic church a problem arose because some of the members were buying and eating meat that had been sacrificed to heathen gods. In itself there was nothing wrong with eating such meat, but some of the weak members were disturbed by such a practice. They could not forget that the meat had been used in the heathen sacrifices, and it troubled them to eat that meat. So Paul instructed the Christians, "All food is clean, but it is wrong for a man to eat anything that causes someone else to stumble. It is better not to eat meat or drink wine or to do anything else that will cause your brother to fall" (Romans 14:20,21).

By encouraging the Christians not to eat the meat that was offered to idols, Paul was stating a general principle: Don't do anything that might cause the Christian who is weak in his faith and understanding to fall into sin and from the faith. If a person has some doubts as to whether something is right or wrong and does it anyway—but not from faith—he is sinning, for "everything that does not come from faith is sin" (Romans 14:23). For example, a pastor may refrain from visiting the local bar because some weak member who has a drinking problem may see him and say to himself, "If the pastor does it, so can I," knowing full well that his own drinking of an alcoholic beverage would most often lead to drunkenness. The pastor refrains, knowing that such a person would be in grave danger of losing his faith.

Exercise of freedom needed

But there are other times when the church must insist on exercising its Christian freedom. Such a time occurred during the Reformation. The Lutheran reformers and the theologians of the Roman Catholic Church had some serious doctrinal differences, differences that went to the very heart of the gospel message. The Catholic Church taught then, and still does today, that a sinner is *not* saved through faith in Christ alone but still must perform good works in order to enter heaven.[9] The Bible teaches, however, "It is by grace you have been saved, through faith— and this not from yourselves, it is the gift of God—not by works, so that no one can boast" (Ephesians 2:8,9).

At that time there were also differences between the Lutherans and the Catholics concerning what were adiaphora and what were not. At one point in the controversy, some Lutherans felt they could begin settling their differences with the Roman church by acceding to the demands of the Catholics and adopting certain Catholic rites and ceremonies that were not forbidden in the Bible. But the faithful confessors insisted that in times of doctrinal controversy, when those who held to the truth of God's Word were being persecuted, it was wrong for them to give up their Christian liberty in such matters. It was no longer an adiaphoron, they contended, when the gospel was at stake.

That scriptural position is recorded in our Lutheran Confessions: "In time of persecution, when a clear-cut confession is demanded of us, we dare not yield to the enemies in such indifferent things. . . . In such a case it is no longer a question of indifferent things, but a matter which has to do with the truth of the gospel, Christian liberty, and the sanctioning of public idolatry, as well as preventing offense to the weak in the faith. In all these things we have no concessions to make, but we should witness an unequivocal confession and suffer in consequence what God sends us and what he lets the enemies inflict on us."[10]

Adiaphora and Bible translations

A contemporary example of dealing with adiaphora could be in the matter of a Bible translation. For many years our congregations used the King James Version of the Bible, and some still do. Although it was written in the English of another time, it was a reliable translation. In recent years some felt that the church could be served better if a contemporary Bible translation were used in our Christian literature, which would especially aid in teaching God's Word to our children. After a thorough study of many Bible translations on the market, the New International Version was chosen for use in our Christian literature, such as our church periodicals and our educational materials. Still, each congregation can decide which translation it wants to use.

In some churches the congregation allowed the pastor to make the decision regarding which translation he would read from the lectern. In other congregations the voters' assembly made the decision. It was all a matter of Christian liberty.

But, let us say, a controversy arose in the congregation concerning the use of a Bible translation. The congregation was divided. One group felt that the congregation should continue to use the King James Version. Another group wanted to use the New International Version. Again, the different translations would be discussed by the congregation so that a God-pleasing decision could be made. Since the matter is an adiaphoron, a number of different decisions might be made, and each one would be God-pleasing. A vote could be taken, and whatever decision was made, the membership would abide by it.

In some cases, however, some may be weak in their understanding and doubt that changing to a different translation is the right thing to do. For the sake of those members, the congregation may decide to stay with the traditional translation, at least for the time being. This decision will be followed by instructing the membership on Bible translations in general and contemporary translations in particular. Such instruction will be done especially for the sake of those who are weak in their understanding of Bible translations.

However, if after such instruction some go so far as to say that it is wrong to use anything but a certain translation of the Bible, the congregation is no longer dealing with members who are weak in their understanding but who are persisting in error. Then, as the church fathers did before, we should explain that it is no longer an adiaphoron. Now the truth is at stake, and the translation the congregation has decided to use will be the one employed by the congregation.

Summary

The following scriptural principles should be kept in mind in matters of adiaphora in regard to the church:

1. The church enjoys freedom from all types of ceremonial laws. It is, therefore, free to establish its own forms of organization, worship, and ministry.

2. The church should exercise its Christian liberty in a way that does not disturb its unity but in a way that glorifies God.

3. The church should refrain from using its Christian liberty when such freedom may cause the weak Christian to sin.

4. The church should refuse to use its freedom when the truth of God's Word is at stake.

The apostle Paul summarized the right way and the proper spirit for exercising our Christian freedom when he wrote, "'Everything is permissible'—but not everything is beneficial. 'Everything is permissible'—but not everything is constructive. Nobody should seek his own good, but the good of others" (1 Corinthians 10:23,24).

9

Freedom for Daily Living

"Dad, may I use the car tonight?" asked the 16-year-old who had just received his driver's license.

The father loved his son and knew that he had displayed good driving skills and judgment. But he wondered how it would be when his son was driving the car and picking up his friends. Would the boy be tempted to act foolishly when behind the wheel? Would he have an accident? What should the father answer? It's not an easy decision to make, and we cannot get an answer by thumbing through the pages of the Bible.

Gospel and law

It is true that the more we study the Bible, the better we understand God's will for our lives. God wants us to hear his Word, where his unconditional love for us is revealed. He wants us to learn of his Son, whom he sent into the world to save us. And we do believe that Christ has redeemed us and secured our place in heaven.

In response to his love, God wants us to live a life that reflects our love for him. Thus he has given us his law to guide us in our day-to-day living as Christians. When we have to make decisions concerning right and wrong, the first question we should ask ourselves is, "What would God want me to do?" And often we find the answer in his holy law. His unchanging Word makes such decisions relatively easy for the Christian.

Adiaphora

But there are many times in our life when decisions have to be made and the Bible does not offer some ready-made answer. For example, God did tell his believers in the Old Testament what they could and could not eat. But the freedom that we enjoy as New Testament believers includes freedom to choose any kind of food that will nourish our bodies. The only rule for our eating and drinking is that it should be done in moderation.

Some may assume that they as Christians have free rein to do as they please in anything that God has not mentioned in his Word. Nothing is further from the truth. That could lead to selfish decisions that appeal to the sinful flesh and are not in accordance with God's will. Rather, Jesus has some sound advice that certainly applies in general to every facet of our Christian life. "Be as shrewd as snakes and as innocent as doves" (Matthew 10:16). God has given us a mind. Because of the Fall, it is sinful by nature, but since our conversion our mind has now also been sanctified. Such a reasoning mind will aid us in making sound judgments that will please our Lord. And there are scriptural principles that will guide our thinking and decision making in matters about which God has not specifically said yes or no.

We have discussed adiaphora in the previous chapter. There we applied the principles to decisions a congregation must often make. Now we will see how those same principles should be applied to our lives as individual Christians who, at times, have tough choices to make.

In 1 Corinthians 6:12, the apostle Paul wrote, " 'Everything is permissible for me'—but not everything is beneficial." Here the apostle is referring to matters that God has neither commanded nor forbidden in his law. Paul is not speaking of things that would benefit him personally, but rather he is speaking for the good of those with whom he has some association and contact. There will be times when we enjoy the freedom we have through Christ, and we will do what we think is right. And there will be other times when we must take into consideration what effect our words and actions might have on others.

Causing offense

Paul is referring to the latter when he warns, "Be careful . . . that the exercise of your freedom does not become a stumbling block to the weak" (1 Corinthians 8:9). The apostle is not speaking about an inadvertent fall that still permits someone to get up, brush himself off, and go on his way. He is talking about something far more serious. The word *stumble* means deathtrap, a kind of trap that snares animals and kills them. In the spiritual realm it refers to a stumbling that could easily result in falling away from the faith.

The apostle is telling us how we should deal with those who are weak in their faith. They have not as yet gained a mature understanding of all that God has to say to them in his Word. They may not be certain whether something is right or wrong in the eyes of God. Thus they could easily take offense at something that we say or do, an offense so serious that it could cause them to abandon the faith and be eternally lost.

On his second missionary journey, Paul founded a congregation in Corinth. Later, in his letters to this congregation, he addressed some serious problems that had arisen after he had left. One of the difficulties had to do with the kind of food the members were eating.

Some of the best steaks in Corinth were purchased at the market that sold meat that had previously been used in idol worship. God did not forbid the eating of such meat, but some of the Christians were still bothered by those who were eating this meat, for they knew that it had been used for heathen sacrifices. Paul encouraged the more mature Christians, therefore, to refrain from purchasing and eating the meat sacrificed to idols, lest they offend the weak. Paul did not want them to sin against their brother's or sister's erring conscience. He did not want the weak to forsake the Christian faith.

On one occasion my family could have been guilty of offending the new wife of our nephew. She was of Jewish descent and a recent convert to Christianity. We invited the couple for dinner, and my wife served them a pork roast. Not until the next day did it occur to us that we could have caused offense. In weakness of faith our guest might not have been certain that it was right for her to eat such meat. She ate it, but perhaps she had eaten it with a weak and troubled conscience. The Bible teaches that whatever is not done in faith is sin. We learned later that she was not offended by our choice of menu, so no offense was given.

It would certainly have been wrong for us to try to convince our nephew's wife to eat the meat if she had refused to eat it. We might have tried to show her from the New Testament that Christ has fulfilled all of the Old Testament ceremonial laws and that there is, therefore, nothing wrong in eating pork. And if she had eaten it, not fully understanding and being convinced that it was an adiaphoron, she would have sinned against her conscience, and we would have been guilty of causing offense.

Weakness of faith

The Bible has this to say in such matters: "Accept him whose faith is weak, without passing judgment on disputable matters. One man's faith allows him to eat everything, but another man, whose faith is weak, eats only vegetables" (Romans 14:1,2).

The Bible does not encourage us to think of ourselves as the strong Christian and of many others in our fellowship as the weak Christians. Such an attitude smacks of haughtiness and pride. All of us have our weaknesses, more than we are ready to admit. All of us, even the most faithful, have given in to our sinful flesh and done things that we later realized were wrong.

Abraham is called the father of all believers. He was truly a man of God, yet he displayed weaknesses of faith. When Abraham took his family into Egypt, he passed Sarah off as his sister because he was afraid of what Pharaoh would do to him in order to get Sarah as his wife. Another time he tried to help God keep his promise of a son by having a child with Sarah's maidservant, Hagar.

And yet the Bible tells us, "By faith Abraham, even though he was past age—and Sarah herself was barren—was enabled to become a father because he considered him faithful who had made the promise" (Hebrews 11:11). Even though Abraham had moments of weakness, he remained a man of faith.

Drinking alcoholic beverages

A Christian may also have an erring conscience. He may trust in Jesus Christ as his Savior but think that certain things are sinful when, in fact, they are not. For example, some Christians are taught in their churches that drinking alcoholic beverages is sinful. If we know that a person is opposed to strong drink, we should not flaunt our Christian liberty by indulging ourselves when he is present. Instead, if we should happen to have him as our guest, we will choose not to serve anything that may offend him.

Or take the example of a person who is an alcoholic. He knows that the Bible does not forbid drinking alcohol, and so over the years he has indulged himself. In fact, he has been guilty of repeated drunkenness and has become addicted to alcohol. But now he is a "recovering alcoholic," living in daily repentance as a Christian. Even though he knows the Bible does not forbid drinking, it is not an adiaphoron for him because even one drink may lead to the sin of intoxication. Not wanting to be "mastered by anything" except Christ (1 Corinthians 6:12), he will, with the help of God, refrain from drinking. In this way he is living his freedom in Christ.

In the presence of these two people, we may choose to do exactly the same thing as they do—refrain from drinking alcohol. For us it is an adiaphoron; for them it is not.

For the one, to drink would be sinning against his erring, weak conscience; for the other, to drink at all may lead to the sin of drunkenness.

Gambling

Many forms of gambling have been legalized in recent years. The lottery has swept over the United States. Bingo had been restricted to some charitable institutions, but lately bingo halls have sprung up all over the country, especially on Indian reservations.

Strange as it may seem, the Bible does not categorically state that games of chance are wrong. And Christians are tempted to take advantage of such silence on the part of God. While the various forms of gambling are not forbidden in the Scriptures, God does issue warnings. In fact, two of his Ten Commandments begin with the words, "You shall not covet." Greed can easily possess the heart, and it can take on many forms. "The love of money is a root of all kinds of evil" (1 Timothy 6:10), the Scriptures warn. And one of those evils might be gambling. This "fun activity" may turn into an addiction.

When I was working my way through school, selling door-to-door in the suburban area of Chicago, I sat next to a man at a lunch counter one Saturday. He was quite nervous because the service was not as prompt as he wanted it. He told me he was in a hurry to get to the Arlington racetrack. The week before, his bets had paid off, and he was eager to make some more money.

On another occasion I was in a lawyer's office, getting advice on the purchase of our first church property, when the phone ring. After the attorney hung up, he said that was one of his clients who was trying to kick his gambling habit. He called to say that once again he had lost his shirt. For such individuals, games of chance are not adiaphora. As in the case of the drug addict, their gambling controls and ruins their lives.

When tempted to participate in a game of chance, we do well to ask ourselves the questions: Why am I doing this? Is this good stewardship of what God has entrusted to me?

Our bodies a temple

What about smoking? It has customarily been considered an adiaphoron. But in recent years we have had some questions about it. The medical profession has demonstrated that smoking, as well as secondhand smoke, can be injurious to our health. While we cannot say that smoking in itself is sin, as Christians we are reminded, "Do you not know that your body is a temple of the Holy Spirit, who is in you, whom you have received from God? You are not your own; you were bought at a price. Therefore honor God with your body" (1 Corinthian 6:19,20). These words apply to every facet of our Christian lives. We should be mindful of them when considering adiaphora.

The reminder that we have been bought with the holy, precious blood of God's own Son should prompt us to honor God with the way we treat our bodies. Sin has corrupted them and made them weak and subject to illness. But our bodies have been redeemed at a great price. And we honor God with our bodies when we take care of our health in a reasonable and wholesome way. Moderation is the key word here.

How do we know whether or not something that is not mentioned in the Bible is good for us or not. Ask yourself this simple question: "Can I take it or leave it?" When you can give an honest "yes" to that question, then for you it is an adiaphoron.

Insisting on Christian freedom

There may be occasions when we will insist on exercising our Christian liberty, when the truth of the gospel is at stake. For example, a weak Christian becomes an erring Christian when he not only refrains from using alcoholic beverages but tries to tell us that to drink them is a sin. Since the Bible does not forbid it, we cannot even leave the impression that we agree with his error. When that happens, we will exercise our Christian liberty and have an occasional drink, even though he may be offended by it. He is taking offense when he shouldn't. We are not giving offense; we are giving witness to our Christian liberty.

Some people will take offense, especially when we proclaim the gospel. The Jews were offended at the message of Jesus and the apostles that they were saved by God's grace alone and not by their good works. They stubbornly held to the falsehood that obedience to the law made people right with God. For them, the preaching of the cross became a stumbling block, a deathtrap, that finally destroyed both body and soul in hell.

We cannot prevent people from taking offense by what we teach and the kind of life we lead. We are not at fault when errorists are offended by what we believe and what we do in accordance with God's Word. Again we are reminded of Paul's admonition, "It is for freedom that Christ has set us free. Stand firm, then, and do not let yourselves be burdened again by a yoke of slavery" (Galatians 5:1).

Love, the guiding principle

As Christians we will always have difficult choices to make. But there is one word that God wants us to use that will guide our actions—LOVE. We have a tendency to think only of ourselves and what will be good for us. In the last seven commandments God instructs us how to show love for our neighbor. But he does not prescribe rules for all of our actions. Instead, the Bible states a general truth, "Nobody should seek his own good, but the good of others" (1 Corinthians 10:24). Certainly God wants us to take care of our own needs. We are not to make this our preoccupation, however, so that we neglect others or do not put others first. God wants us to keep the welfare of our neighbor constantly in mind. That is why the last seven commandments are summarized with the words, "Love your neighbor as yourself." The question we should be asking ourselves is not, "What would I like to do?" but "What will benefit others?" For "love is kind . . . not self-seeking" (1 Corinthians 13:4,5).

That word *love* can be a rather nebulous term. We will debate at times about the best way to show love. When we pray to God for his help, when we put others ahead of ourselves, when we are motivated by Christ's love for us, we will begin to show proper love for others.

One important way to show such love is to patiently instruct the weak. When a person has a weak and faulty understanding of the Bible, we can perform no greater act of love for him than to lead him into the truths of God's Word. The Bible will give him a richer understanding of God's will and, by God's grace and the Spirit's power, will strengthen his Christian faith. He will learn that some things that he thought God allows are, in fact, sinful. And he will realize that some things he thought were wrong are, in fact, not sinful at all. Acting as instruments of God, we can help our fellow believers overcome such weaknesses in their faith.

Summary

The above are only a few examples of adiaphora. We could not possibly list them all or try to anticipate everything that might come up in our lives. But it is clear from the Scriptures that God wants us to use our Christian freedom wisely in those areas where he has not given us specific instructions.

To summarize, the following scriptural principles in matters of adiaphora should be kept in mind:

1. We should forego our Christian liberty when it may offend the weak Christian, a person who has a doubting or erring conscience.

2. We should not exercise our Christian liberty when it threatens to enslave us.

3. We should exercise our Christian freedom when someone insists something is a sin when it is not.

4. Christian love is the guiding principle in our relationships with others.

Keeping these blessed truths in mind, we will be exercising our Christian freedom the way God intended it to be used.

10

Freedom Enjoyed

The doctrine of Christian freedom is a paradox. In his treatise "The Freedom of a Christian," Luther stated it this way:

A Christian is a perfectly free lord of all, subject to none.

A Christian is a perfectly dutiful servant of all, subject to all.[11]

The Christian life is also a paradox. The Bible describes us as "sorrowful, yet always rejoicing" (2 Corinthians 6:10).

Even though we are God's children and followers of Christ, our life is no bed of roses. We not only have hardships and heartaches that are common to all people; we also have a cross that we bear because we are Christians. We feel the hatred the world has for the gospel when we confess our faith through our words and actions.

Sorrow over our sins plagues us every day. At times we may even feel worthless and have a hard time persevering. At such times we should focus on the freedom we have through Christ, freedom from the grievous burden of the law, freedom from the guilt of our sins, from the slavery of Satan, and from the constant fear of death. Those freedoms Christ has won for us to enjoy. Being free in Christ gives us a fresh start every day and brings joy to our lives.

Joy in our salvation

We may experience many temporal joys of life: a promotion at work, the birth of a new son or daughter, receiving an inheritance, seeing our children succeed in life, or enjoying the company of friends. But none of these gives us our greatest joy. Rather, with David of old we exclaim, "My heart rejoices in your salvation" (Psalm 13:5). That's the salvation that was eternally planned for us and accomplished by Christ's mission on earth. Through his salvation we have been freed from the controlling influence of sin, for we have been freely forgiven by God. Through his salvation we are free from the clutches of the devil; we are no longer under his control. Through Christ's salvation we see his vacated tomb and know that some day our grave will be empty too. Through his free and full salvation we no longer are frustrated trying to set things right with God by obeying his commandments. And at the urging of God's Word, we find pleasure in leading a life according to his holy will. Contemplating these truths only brings joy into our hearts and lives.

Joy in the Word

David leads us in expressing another joy. "I rejoiced with those who said to me, 'Let us go to the house of the LORD'" (Psalm 122:1). Going to church is not a drudgery when we contemplate what takes place in the church service. There we hear of our God's unconditional love for us. In the sermon we learn again and again of Christ's great sacrifice for us. This is the same old gospel that is new to us every time we hear of Jesus' love. We confess our sins and receive God's pardon, and we are privileged to sing God's praises and speak to him with our prayers. Those who delight in God's Word look forward to going to the church where we join fellow believers in worshiping our Savior-God.

Joy in fellowship

A special bond is formed by the Holy Spirit among those who gather together in the church. There we have formed a wonderful relationship with our fellow believers and enjoy their Christian fellowship. There we are able to encourage one another and build each other up in the faith. Through this spiritual bond we are able to share one another's burdens and offer our prayers for those who need them. In our congregation we are able to form friendships that are especially strong and lasting because of our common trust in Christ.

As a pastor I always felt there was a closeness between my members and me that was hard to describe. A pastor always has his people in mind. After I left a congregation that I had served since its founding, I would think almost daily of someone and wonder how he or she was doing. I know how the apostle Paul felt when he wrote to the congregation he had started in Philippi. "In all my prayers for all of you, I always pray with joy because of your partnership in the gospel from the first day until now" (Philippians 1:4,5).

A pastor can easily observe a bond of fellowship among his members. The concerns they express for each other, the help they give one another in time of need, the way they strengthen one another in the faith, and the joy they experience in one another's company all reflect that common bond of faith that is unique among Christians. When we rejoice in the Lord, we also find joy in the company of his believers.

Joy in giving

One of the most common complaints people have against the church is that it is always asking for money. One church member had that view. When her pastor admonished her for not hearing God's Word and receiving the Sacrament, she remained unrepentant, trying to defend herself by claiming, "The church is always asking for money." She had failed to see that her gifts to the church would have been an expression of her love for the Savior.

Our own old Adam, however, is also stingy. Only our new person in Christ looks upon any appeal to support the work of the church and its mission endeavors as an important aspect of living the faith. God has given us the opportunity to express the joy we have because we are free through Christ by letting the "how much" and the "when to give" up to us. He wants our giving to him, to his church, and to others to be an offering that is truly freewill and a giving that is done gladly. Haven't we thanked the Lord for the opportunity to bring our gifts to the Lord? Haven't we found joy in expressing our love for him who first loved us? That is freedom enjoyed.

Have you ever had the feeling that you and only a few others were doing all the work that had to be done in the congregation? Instead of feeling sorry for ourselves, we should be thankful for the many opportunities for service that God is giving us. Instead of going about certain duties with a heavy heart because so many others could be helping and are not, we should find joy in the time we give for him who gave his all for us. The special gifts and talents he has given us are there for us to use to God's glory and for the welfare of others. Whatever responsibility we have been given in the church, we enjoy doing it because we have been made free in Christ.

Joy in witnessing

Do you enjoy witnessing to others concerning your faith? All Christians have been called to be his witnesses here on earth. The Bible gives us this word of encouragement: "Always be prepared to give an answer to everyone who asks you to give the reason for the hope that you have. But do this with gentleness and respect" (1 Peter 3:15). We have a sure and certain hope of salvation because God has made his promise to us in the Scriptures. And our God is a God who is able and willing to keep his promises.

We are not to keep that hope to ourselves, but we are to share it with others. We will want to be prepared to witness to others. We know God's plan of salvation and believe that God wants all sinners to repent of their sins and be saved. We *can* make a simple witness of our faith to those who will listen to us. Afraid? All of us are at one time or another. But when we speak God's truth in love, when the gospel opens the eyes and heart of someone, "there is rejoicing in the presence of the angels of God" (Luke 15:10). Nothing should make us happier except, of course, our own soul's salvation. Both the witness and the convert are filled with joy, for another sinner has been set free by testimony to God's saving Word.

Joy in an ungodly world

Can we really enjoy our Christian freedom when our eyes see and our ears hear so much bad news every day? Every kind of evil and corruption seems to be the order of the day. Sin is no different today from what it has always been.

The pages of the Old Testament are filled with the story of God's people abandoning him for the idolatry of their heathen neighbors. St. Paul had to contend with every kind of immorality when he preached the gospel in Corinth. Luther was shocked by the wickedness of the clergy when he visited Rome. We are appalled when we see how the many false teachers are deceiving so many people today.

But one sign of the end times gives us joy—the gospel is being preached in the whole world. Most recently the iron curtain has been lifted, and we have been able to send our missionaries into parts of Europe today that were closed to us a few years ago. Some of those who had been political slaves for most of their lives have learned that the good news of Jesus Christ has freed them from sin and has saved them. Such freedom they will always be able to enjoy as long as they keep the faith, no matter what system of government they have to live under.

Our God is in the heavens and does whatever pleases him. Our Lord Jesus is at the right hand of God today, ruling the world for our benefit. That should bring us comfort and joy no matter how terrible conditions in the world become.

These conditions will get worse as the number of days left in this world decreases. Jesus is preparing us for the worst when he warns that hatred for the gospel and its messengers will increase. If we should be persecuted because of our faith, the apostles have shown us the way to deal with it. They were imprisoned for preaching God's Word; they were beaten, threatened, and released, but they left, "rejoicing because they had been counted worthy of suffering disgrace for the Name [Jesus]" (Acts 5:41).

Joy in the home

Have you found joy in your home, in your marriage? Maybe such a question will conjure up thoughts of some bad experiences, for not even the best of Christian homes is spared serious problems. When both spouses, however, share a common faith in Christ and practice their religion on a daily basis, they experience peace and contentment and joy. A Christian couple is a daily source of encouragement for one another, and they know how to pray the Fifth Petition, "Forgive us our sins, as we forgive those who sin against us," because their lives and their relationship are far from perfect. The wife remembers the scriptural injunction, "Submit to your [husband] as to the Lord. For the husband is the head of the wife as Christ is the head of the church, his body, of which he is the Savior." And the husband hears God say, "Love your [wife], just as Christ loved the church and gave himself up for her" (Ephesians 5:22-25). They know and believe that Christ has freed them from sin, and that motivates them to love one another as husband and wife should.

For the Christian who is not married or whose spouse does not believe in Christ, there will still be joy in knowing that the most faithful friend a person can have is Jesus. He is a constant companion. His unwavering love is a source of strength in a life that may have many disappointments.

I know of a Christian wife and mother who married someone who was not a member of the church. Repeatedly she asked her husband to attend the pastor's Bible information class, with no response. Finally, she gave up trying. Then one day he came home and announced, "I am going to church this Sunday. I am being confirmed." Because he worked unusual hours, his wife did not realize that he had been attending the pastor's class. Now they are in church regularly, attending Bible classes, and taking an active part in the work of the church. Today there is real joy in that home.

Joy in raising children

We thank God that he has given us our children and made them his own through Baptism. They are both our children and God's. He not only wants us to clothe and feed them; he also has called us to raise them to honor and respect his Word. Some of the most important times parents have with their children are when they teach them about their Savior, help them understand and learn their catechism, and say their prayers together at night. Although such training and instructing seems somewhat routine when it is done year after year, those children will not forget what their parents have done for them.

One Christian couple had a model Christian home. The Lord had blessed them with an abundance of material things and six children. They gave their children a Christian education at home and in school. When their children grew up and established their own homes, they did not forget what their parents had done for them spiritually. At the couple's 50th wedding anniversary, all of their children and grandchildren sang, from memory, all five verses of "Now the Light Has Gone Away," a hymn their mother and grandmother had taught them.

Parents are happy when their children are healthy, when they do well in school, when they show respect for their elders, and when they are successful in what they are doing. But nothing brings greater joy to Christian parents than to see that their children have kept the faith and, in turn, are teaching it to their children. Our joy in the freedom Christ has won for us is a joy that can be shared and multiplied through our family. And that sharing begins at home.

Joy in old age

Old age brings days that are good and days that are not so good. Very often we gauge the kind of day we have by how we feel. Modern medicine has extended our life span, but it has also increased the amount of time we spend in the hospital and at the doctor's office. And yet each day we measure as another 24 hours of God's grace.

As we get older we are able to do things that we found too little time to do when we were young. We spend more time meditating on the Word and on the promises of our Lord. Life takes on a little different perspective as we get older. More and more thoughts are heavenly, with an increasing realization that worldly matters are relatively unimportant.

After one retires, he or she can still find many opportunities for service, none of which is more important than witnessing to the freedom we have through Christ. We pray, "Even when I am old and gray, do not forsake me, O God, till I declare your power to the next generation, your might to all who are to come" (Psalm 71:18). The Lord will not forsake us when we grow old. If we do have a few more days left, we can use them to tell our children and grandchildren how marvelously God has used his power to overcome all spiritual enemies. As we get older we realize that we can give our descendants no better legacy than the gospel of Jesus Christ. Many of us remember parents and grandparents who, by word and example, proclaimed the joy of free and full salvation to us. If they left us an inheritance of worldly things, these are here today and gone tomorrow, but the confession of their faith and their witness to the truth of God's Word have made a lasting impression on us. We thank God for our forefathers who were the first to teach us what freedom in Christ was really all about. And when it is our turn, we should welcome the opportunity to witness.

Old age, then, is not sitting around waiting for death. Even the bedridden are able to offer up their prayers to the throne of grace, prayers that they know their heavenly Father will hear and answer. The psalmist has an interesting way of describing the sunset years as productive ones. "They will still bear fruit in old age, they will stay fresh and green, proclaiming, 'The LORD is upright; he is my Rock, and there is no wickedness in him'" (Psalm 92:14,15). At the very time in life when we may be tempted to think that there is little for us to do, God describes us as trees that still bear fruit, as people who are still "fresh and green," for we are able to proclaim to anyone who will listen that the Lord is the Rock of our salvation.

If we happen to live in a retirement community or a rest home, opportunities to witness for Christ are at our door. A former Lutheran elementary school teacher retired and moved to an apartment complex reserved for senior citizens. Soon he was conducting a Bible class there. One of his neighbors who attended wanted to hear more. Over a period of months he unfolded God's plan of salvation to her by expounding the gospel of Luke. One day she confessed her faith in Christ and asked to be baptized. After consulting with his pastor, they agreed that the one who had instructed her should do the baptizing. So he baptized her, and another sinner was set free by an elderly Christian's witness. Our life of serving the Lord is never over until the Lord determines that it is over.

Perfect joy anticipated

And when it is over, we will experience a perfect joy. We will be with the Lord forever. It is hard for us to imagine a time and place where there will be nothing to dampen our Christian joy. Even though we believe in Christ, while we are on this earth we experience the headaches and heartaches of life. But that will change.

Soon we will no longer be troubled daily by our sins and those of others. Soon we will not have to battle the wily temptations of the devil. Soon we will no longer be thinking of our last hour on earth, for soon we will fully realize how perfectly and completely Christ has freed us from all things sinful and temporal.

The Bible has only given us a glimpse of what eternal life will be like. How can heavenly things be adequately described with earthly words? But the Holy Spirit has inspired enough words on the pages of Scripture to give us an understanding that someday we will be living in a new heaven and a new earth with our Savior-God in eternal bliss. With a glorified body we will see our glorified Lord. Today we know him by faith; tomorrow we will see him face-to-face for all eternity. In heaven we will be filled with joy in God's presence, and we will experience pleasures with him that will never end (Psalm 16:11).

A bird builds a new nest every year. There it will lay its eggs, hatch its young, and feed them until they can fly on their own. But that creature knows its nest is only a temporary home. Earth is only our temporary home; we are only visitors here; our real home is the one that Christ has prepared for us by his redeeming work.

Christ has earned for us a permanent place in heaven, so that we may enjoy his company forever. What perfect and joyous freedom awaits us there!

Endnotes

[1]*Great Movie Themes* (Milwaukee: Hal Leonard Corporation, 1995).

[2]Leon Uris, *Exodus*, p. 626.

[3]*Milwaukee Sentinel*, February 28, 1995.

[4]Martin Luther, *What Luther Says: An Anthology*, compiled by Ewald M. Plass (St. Louis: Concordia Publishing House, 1959), Vol. 1, p. 491.

[5]In addition to John 15:13,14, note the following Bible passages: "You see, at just the right time, when we were still powerless, Christ died for the ungodly. Very rarely will anyone die for a righteous man, though for a good man someone might possibly dare to die. But God demonstrates his own love for us in this: While we were still sinners, Christ died for us" (Romans 5:6-8). "This is love: not that we loved God, but that he loved us and sent his Son as an atoning sacrifice for our sins" (1 John 4:10).

[6]Roland H. Bainton, *The Martin Luther Christmas Book* (Philadelphia: The Westminster Press, 1948), p. 38.

[7]In its official catechism, the Roman Catholic Church states: "The Church, to whom the transmission and interpretation of Revelation is entrusted, 'does not derive her certainty about

all revealed truths from the holy Scriptures alone. Both Scripture and Tradition must be accepted and honored with equal sentiments of devotion and reverence'" (*Catechism of the Catholic Church* [Washington: United States Catholic Conference, 1994], par. 82).

[8]The Mormon religion "rules out the use of liquor, tobacco, and 'hot drinks' (which have been officially interpreted as tea and coffee). In a recent survey of LDS youth the #1 sin was breaking the Word of Wisdom [an important part of Mormonism's "scriptures"]; sexual immorality came in #5 . . . A Mormon must keep the Word of Wisdom in order to be temple-worthy" (Mark J. Cares, *Speaking the Truth in Love to Mormons* [Milwaukee: Northwestern Publishing House, 1993], p. 279).

[9]At the Council of Trent, the Roman Catholic Church officially condemned the biblical doctrine that we are saved by God's grace alone through faith in Christ Jesus without any effort on our part. "If anyone says that justifying faith is nothing else than trust in divine mercy, which remits sins for Christ's sake, or that it is this trust alone by which we are justified, let him be anathema [accursed]" (Martin Chemnitz, *Examination of the Council of Trent*, Part I. [St. Louis: Concordia Publishing House, 1972], p. 551).

[10]Formula of Concord, Epitome, Article X: 6, *The Book of Concord: The Confessions of the Evangelical Lutheran Church*, translated and edited by Theodore G. Tappert (Philadelphia: Fortress Press, 1959), p. 493.

[11]Martin Luther, *Luther's Works*, American Edition, edited by Jaroslav Pelikan and Helmut T. Lehmann (St. Louis: Concordia Publishing House; Philadelphia: Fortress Press, 1958–1986), Vol. 31, p. 344.

For Further Reading

Becker, Siegbert W. "Christian Liberty." Essay at the Forty-seventh Biennial Convention of the Wisconsin Evangelical Lutheran Synod. *Proceedings*, August 1983.

"The Ecclesiastical Rites That Are Called Adiaphora or Things Indifferent." Formula of Concord, Epitome and Solid Declaration, Article X. *The Book of Concord: The Confessions of the Evangelical Lutheran Church*. Translated and edited by Theodore G. Tappert, pp. 492-494, 610-616. Philadelphia: Fortress Press, 1959.

Luther, Martin. "The Freedom of a Christian." *Luther's Works*. American Edition. Vol. 31. Edited by Jaroslav Pelikan and Helmut T. Lehmann. St. Louis: Concordia Publishing House; Philadelphia: Fortress Press, 1958–1986.

Reim, Edmund. "Our Christian Liberty and Its Proper Use." *Our Great Heritage*, Vol. 3. Edited by Lyle W. Lange. Milwaukee: Northwestern Publishing House, 1991.

Scripture Index

2 Timothy
  3:16—15,18

Hebrews
  1:14—74
  2:14,15—79
  4:9,10—69
  11:4—96
  11:11—118

James
  4:7—85

1 Peter
  2:16—43
  3:15—129

  4:11—108
  5:8—75,79

1 John
  2:15—76
  3:8—76-78
  3:15—56

Jude
  6—12,63,75

Revelation
  14:13—98
  20:15—63
  21:4—69

Subject Index